BY THE WIND

Fujian and Northeast Asia

www.royalcollins.com

ILLUSTRATED FUJIAN AND THE MARITIME SILK ROAD

BY THE WIND

Fujian and Northeast Asia

Xu Bin & Zhang Jinhong

Edited by Xie Bizhen

Books Beyond Boundaries

ROYAL COLLINS

By the Wind:
Fujian and Northeast Asia

Xu Bin & Zhang Jinhong
Edited by Xie Bizhen
Translated by Daniel McRyan

First published in 2022 by Royal Collins Publishing Group Inc.
Groupe Publication Royal Collins Inc.
BKM Royalcollins Publishers Private Limited

Headquarters: 550-555 boul. René-Lévesque O Montréal (Québec) H2Z1B1 Canada
India office: 805 Hemkunt House, 8th Floor, Rajendra Place, New Delhi 110 008

ISBN: 978-1-4878-0885-3

Special thanks to the contribution of linguistic consultant Mr. Tomasz Solak with Japanese and Korean primary sources.

To find out more about our publications, please visit www.royalcollins.com.

FOREWORD

As early as the 1st century BC, China had established an entire sea route from Xuwen and Hepu of Guangdong Province in southeastern China to the east coast of India; however, the early Chinese navigation was rarely related to the country's economic development. Emperors launched navigations to seek either the elixir of immortality or overseas treasures to maintain the luxurious and decadent lifestyle in the palace. The real overseas trade of China commenced when the Bureau of Foreign Shipping was set up in the Tang Dynasty. It was not until then that overseas trade was included in the national fiscal revenue.

Thanks to its superior geographical condition, Fujian is destined to play a significant role in the history of the overseas transportation and trade of China.

When the Maritime Silk Road is mentioned today, the descriptions tend to paint an easy and poetic picture. However, the formation of the Maritime Silk Road in history has gone through years of thick and thin. The merciless sea had devoured countless lives before the winding Maritime Silk Road came into being. As we look back on its development, we must not forget those great pioneers, namely, the monks who crossed the sea, the common people who went to sea to scrape out a living, the soldiers who went to war abroad, the envoys who were sent overseas, the courtiers who took refuge in foreign countries, the survivors of the shipwrecks, and the crew of Zheng He, who led seven voyages to the West.

It was commonly believed that Fujian ships were the best of all in the Song Dynasty. It was because Fujian had the most advanced navigation and shipbuilding technology of the time that the Quanzhou port had tremendous prosperity. The compass was widely used in navigation and nautical astronomy was developed. The stars were the guide and the wind the fuel. Navigation guidebooks were written and maps were drawn and passed down for generations. The advanced Western technology was also widely adopted in the navigation of Fujian sailors, such as the hourglass and the telescope. Their concept of navigation was evolving rapidly. The saying that "the sea is where Fujian people farm" pinpoints that they sailed for economic benefits. And the leverage of the economy drove them to open the age of Chinese exploration, where voyages were made all over the world and goods shipped overseas.

As per the existing historical data, the footprints of Fujian maritime merchants have been found in Japan and the Korean Peninsula, Southeast Asia, South Asian countries and the African continent. Business people from foreign countries also took Fujian ports as their footholds of trade. Historical documents have recorded that foreign merchant vessels trading with Fujian came from Asia, Africa, Europe, and America. The ancient Maritime Silk Road of China was a joint construction by the people of all countries in the world.

We admire the perfection of the ancient Maritime Silk Road, scrutinize the history of the navigation of Fujian sailors, and respect the outstanding contribution of Fujian ancestors to China's navigation. Their extraordinary sailing activities have left us abundant treasure, such as the sunken ships in the deep ocean, the traded goods that were found everywhere, the harbors silent for many years, the vaguely recognizable buoys, the long navigation picture scrolls, the yellowing nautical guide manuals, and the Mazu temples. The compilation of the illustrated series *Fujian and the Maritime Silk Road* aims to gather these scattered historical fragments piece by piece, so that a full picture of the historical record of Fujian on the ancient Maritime Silk Road can be seen.

The history of the development of the ancient Maritime Silk Road has pinpointed that the Maritime Silk Road came into being thanks to both Chinese and the people of various countries and regions along the way. Now, China's proposal to jointly build the Maritime Silk Road of the 21st Century conforms to the trend of world multi-polarization, economic globalization, and social informatization. Conducive to promoting the orderly and free flow of economic elements, it conforms to the fundamental interests of both China and the international community, highlights the common ideal and pursuit of the human society, and will inject positive energy to the world development.

Reviewing the history of Fujian and the Maritime Silk Road enables us to understand that in the process of building the Maritime Silk Road of the 21st Century, China should make an effort to enhance its comprehensive national strength, develop a value system attractive to all countries, create real soft power, and build its international image and prestige, so as to gradually become a strong global influence.

We shall learn from the history of Fujian on the Maritime Silk Road, explore the secret of success, seize the opportunity, stride into a new era with confidence, and create a victorious future.

Xie Bizhen

INTRODUCTION

Fujian, against the mountains and facing the sea, connects Japan, the Korean Peninsula and itself. Ships pass through the waters, leaving and reaching ports, thus forming sea routes, on which the trade of goods has been smooth, the people have been bonding, and culture has been transmitted. This constitutes the Maritime Silk Road between China's coastal areas and Northeast Asian countries. This sea passage has promoted the social and economic development and the progress of civilization in the area.

The Maritime Silk Road in Northeast Asia is a road of friendship jointly built by the people of all Northeast Asian countries. For thousands of years, the people of Fujian, together with the people of Japan and the Korean Peninsula, have gone through good and bad times in opening up this great sea passage in Northeast Asia: it witnessed the exchange of needed goods, the sails of envoys who were sent to establish friendly relations, eminent monks who preached Buddhism and sought classics, and communicators of production skills and cultural knowledge.

History has never forgotten the past events of Fujian and Northeast Asian Maritime Silk Road. The sea has painted every bit of it into a most beautiful picture.

Let's gently go into the gate of history and see how the Maritime Silk Road stretches from Fujian to Japan and to the Korean Peninsula.

CONTENTS

Foreword V

Introduction VII

Chapter 1 Fujianese Opened up the Route to the Korean Peninsula and Japan 1

1 The Early Exchanges Between Fujian and Northeast Asia 2
2 Goryeo Maps and Records 4

Chapter 2 The Monks Who Crossed the Sea 7

1 The Monk Jianzhen crossed the ocean to Japan and Fujian 8
2 The Monk Enchin 10
3 The Monk Kūkai to Fujian 13
4 Ingen founded Ōbaku-shū 17
5 Shilla monks travelling to Fujian 41
6 Friendships between Chinese and Japanese Buddism 43

Chapter 3 The Construction of Northeast Asia Business District by the Fujianese 57

1 Ships Coming from the South 58
2 Thriving Trade 68

3 The Fujian Officials in Goryeo 80
4 The Zheng Family and Japan 82
5 Legend of Chinese Business People in Nagasaki 90

CHAPTER 4 SHIPS, PORTS, AND SEA ROUTES 95

1 The Busy Ships 96
2 Clamoring Harbors 106
3 The Endless Sea 117

CHAPTER 5 THE MINGLING OF COMMERCE AND CULTURE 125

1 Various Trade Goods 126
2 Books and Woodblock Printing Technique 141

SUMMARY 171

REFERENCES 173

CHAPTER 1

FUJIANESE OPENED UP THE ROUTE TO THE KOREAN PENINSULA AND JAPAN

Historically, a large number of Chinese northerners migrated southward to Fujian, which brought not only an indispensable labor force to the economic development of the province, but also advanced production technology and culture of the northern region. This contributed to the great progress in all aspects of the Fujian society. Since the middle period of the Tang Dynasty, two coastal cities, Quanzhou and Fuzhou, have risen rapidly, receiving a considerable number of foreign business people. They have therefore gradually grown into major ports for foreign trade in southeast coastal areas of China. In addition to the trade with the countries in the South China Sea, Fujian merchant ships also stretched northward to the Korean Peninsula and Japan.

1 The Early Exchanges Between Fujian and Northeast Asia

In the early Han Dynasty, the sea route between Fuzhou and Panyu had come into being. From the Han Dynasty to the Tang Dynasty, as the local economy of Fujian was gradually developed, the early navigation activities began to be documented in literature. That period is characterized by Fujian's opening of a sea route across the East China Sea to Japan and the Korean Peninsula.

During the Three Kingdoms Period, Eastern Wu was committed to the development of maritime transportation.

Since the Tang Dynasty, Fujian's shipbuilding industry grew, forming two shipbuilding centers, Fuzhou and Quanzhou, which gradually became the major ports for foreign maritime transportation and an intermediate hub of the Maritime Silk Road during the Five Dynasties period.

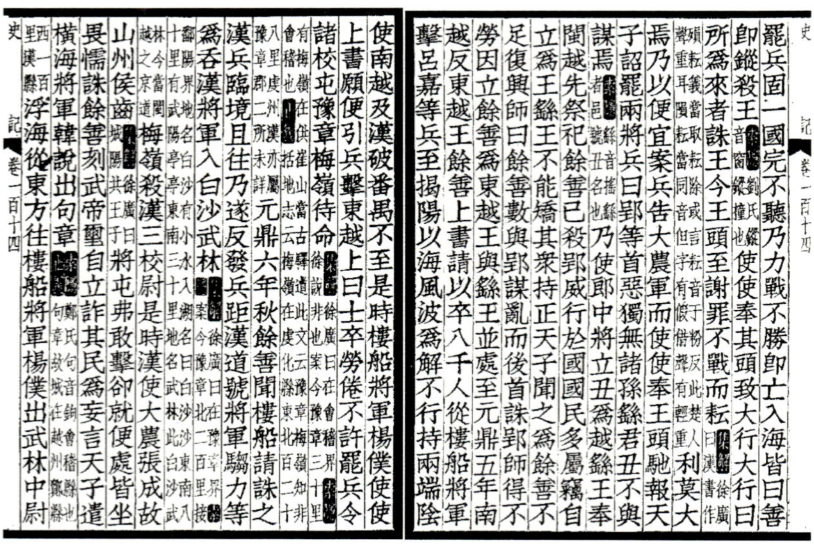
罷兵固一國完不聽乃力戰不勝即亡入海皆曰善
即鏦殺王
使使奉其頭致大行大行曰
所為來者誅王今王頭至謝罪不戰而耘
利莫大
焉乃以便宜案兵告大農軍而使使奉王頭馳報天
子詔罷兩將兵曰郢等首惡獨無諸孫繇君丑不與
謀焉
乃使郎中將立丑為越繇王奉
閩越先祭祀餘善已殺郢威行於國國民多屬竊自
立為王繇王不能矯其衆持正天子聞之為餘善不
足復興師曰餘善數與郢謀亂而後首誅郢師得不
勞因立餘善為東越王與繇王並處至元鼎五年南
越反東越王餘善上書請以卒八千人從樓船將軍
擊呂嘉等兵至揭陽以海風波為解不行持兩端陰
使南越及漢破番禺不至是時樓船將軍楊僕使使
上書願便引兵擊東越上曰士卒勞倦不許罷兵令
諸校屯豫章梅嶺待命
元鼎六年秋餘善聞樓船請誅之
漢兵臨境且往乃遂反發兵距漢道號將軍騶力等
為吞漢將軍入白沙武林
梅嶺殺漢三校尉是時漢使大農張成故
山州侯齒
將屯弗敢擊卻就便處皆坐
畏懦誅餘善刻武帝璽自立詐其民為妄言天子遣
橫海將軍韓說出句章
浮海從東方往樓船將軍楊僕出武林中尉

⊙ *Records of the Historian: Ranked Biographies of Dongyue*, sample pages

府不改館徵上大將軍陸遜輔太子登掌武昌留事

二年春正月魏作合肥新城詔立都講祭酒以教學諸子遣將軍衛溫諸葛直將甲士萬人浮海求夷洲及亶洲亶洲在海中長老傳言秦始皇帝遣方士徐福將童女數千人入海求蓬萊神山及仙藥止此洲不還世相承有數萬家其上人民時有至會稽貨布會稽東縣人海行亦有遭風流移至亶洲者所在絕遠卒不可得至但得夷洲數千人還

⦿ *Records of the Three Kingdoms: Book of Wu*, sample page

2 Goryeo Maps and Records

The maritime communication between Fujian and the Korean Peninsula started in the Tang Dynasty. Fuzhou, located in the middle and lower reaches of the Min River, was the major port.

Goryeo Maps and Records documents many historical facts about Fujian's contacts with the Korean Peninsula.

As per *Goryeo Maps and Records*, the seagoing vessels built in Fujian in the Song Dynasty had a carrying capacity of 360 tons and a displacement of 1000 tons.

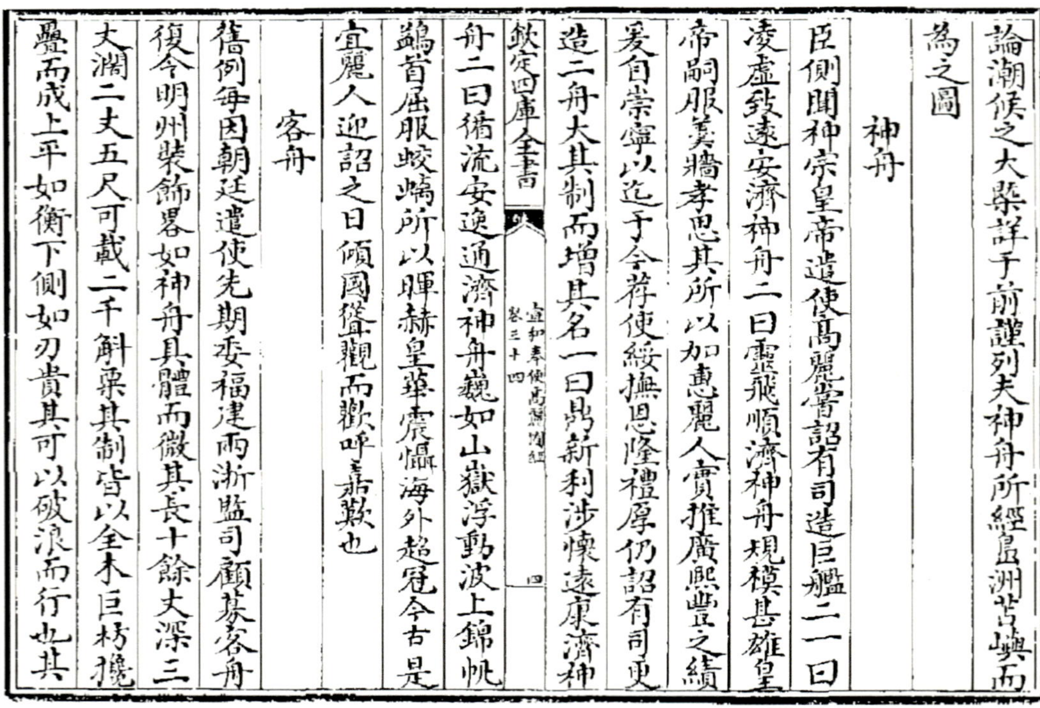
論潮候之大槩詳于前謹列夫神舟所經島洲苫嶼而
為之圖
神舟
臣側聞神宗皇帝遣使高麗嘗詔有司造巨艦二一曰
凌虛致遠安濟神舟二曰靈飛順濟神舟規模甚雄皇
帝嗣服羹牆孝思其所以加惠麗人實推廣熙豐之績
爰自崇寧以迄于今荐使綏撫恩隆禮厚仍詔有司更
造二舟大其制而增其名一曰鼎新利涉懷遠康濟神
欽定四庫全書 宣和奉使高麗圖經 卷三十四 四
舟二曰循流安逸通濟神舟巍如山嶽浮動波上錦帆
鷁首屈服蛟螭所以暉赫皇華震懾海外超冠今古是
宜麗人迎詔之日傾國聳觀而歡呼嘉歎也
客舟
舊例每因朝廷遣使先期委福建兩浙監司顧募客舟
復令明州裝飾畧如神舟具體而微其長十餘丈深三
丈闊二丈五尺可載二千斛粟其制皆以全木巨枋攙
疊而成上平如衡下側如刃貴其可以破浪而行也其

◉ Records of holy boats and passenger boats in *Goryeo Maps and Records*

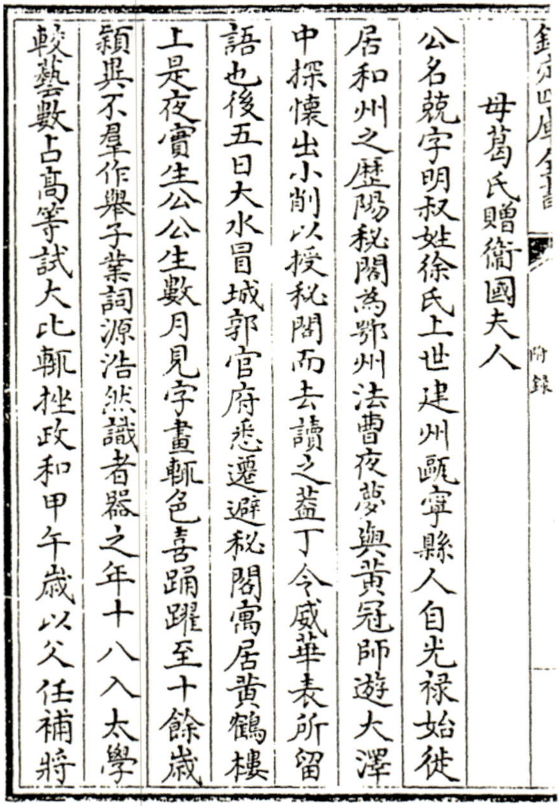

母葛氏贈衛國夫人

公名兢字明叔姓徐氏上世建州甌寧縣人自光祿始徙

居和州之歷陽秘閣為鄂州法曹夜夢與黃冠師遊大澤

中探懷出小削以授秘閣而去讀之蓋丁令威華表所留

語也後五日大水冒城郭官府悉遷避秘閣寓居黃鶴樓

上是夜實生公公生數月見字畫輒色喜踊躍至十餘歲

穎異不羣作舉子業詞源浩然識者器之年十八入太學

較藝數占高等試大比輒挫政和甲午歲以父任補將

⦿ Xu Jing, the author of *Goryeo Maps and Records*

⦿ Seagoing boats in *Goryeo Maps and Records*

CHAPTER 2

THE MONKS WHO CROSSED THE SEA

In the early days of navigation, there were a considerable number of monks who promoted Buddhism and sought Buddhist scriptures. They have made outstanding contributions both to the cause of Buddhism and to that human navigation. Those sailing experiences enabled them to write, translate, and edit Buddhist scriptures, thus leaving many sailing stories of adventure.

1 The Monk Jianzhen crossed the ocean to Japan and Fujian

Monk Jianzhen's six voyages to Japan occupy a significant spot in the history of Buddhist exchanges between China and Japan. Monk Jianzhen was an eminent monk of the Lu Sect in the Tang Dynasty. He was highly accomplished in Buddhism and highly cultivated in medicine and art. He made it to Japan in 754 after six arduous voyages. His preaching of the precepts in Japan gave Japanese Buddhism's precepts a scrupulous new look. He was commended by the Japanese as the founder of Lu Sect of Japanese Buddhism. And his six voyages to spread the Dharma relate to Fujian. The fourth attempt to cross the sea was planned to start from the port of Fuzhou. During the Tang and the Five Dynasties, the prosperity of external transportation of the port of Fuzhou attracted an increasing number of foreign business people and monks.

⦿ Tōshōdaiji Temple was founded by Jianzhen in Japan

⦿ The records of Jianzhen's disciples coming to Fuzhou in the biography of *The Legends of the Eastern Expedition of Jianzhen*

⦿ Records of Jianzhen's disciples who crossed the sea to Japan

2 The Monk Enchin

During the Sui and the Tang Dynasties, Japan sent many envoys and monks to China to learn and absorb China's advanced laws and decrees, Confucian culture, and Buddhist concepts.

Among them, Enchin, a monk who entered China in 853, had an interesting story with Fuzhou. He studied Buddhism in China for five years. After returning to Japan, he preached Esoteric Buddhism widely, becoming the fifth generation leader of the Tendai Sect in Japan. After his death, he was posthumously titled Master Chōshi.

During the late Tang Dynasty and the Five Dynasties, the ruling class of Min (Fuzhou of today) actively supported the spread of Buddhism. Temples were raised and monks recruited in Fujian. The number of temples and monks were ranked top in the country. There were many famous temples (such as Xuefeng (snow peak) Temple in Fuzhou) and eminent monks (such as Shenyan, Shibei, Changqing, et al.). For a time, Fujian was a developed area of Zen beliefs in China.

⊙ Xuefeng Temple in Fuzhou

⦿ The gate of the Kaiyuan Temple in Fuzhou

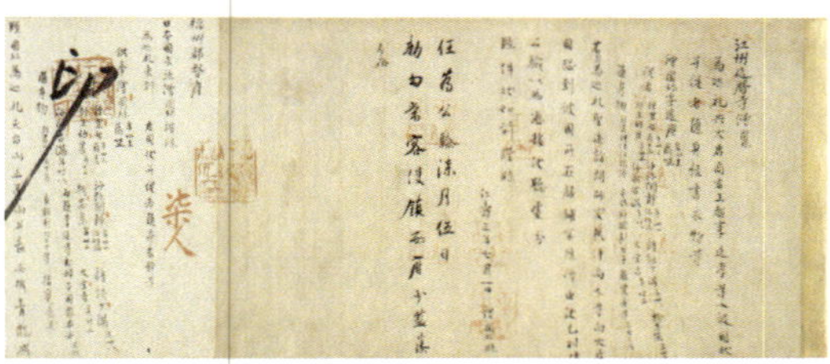

⦿ The first Kugen of Enchin's entry into Tang China

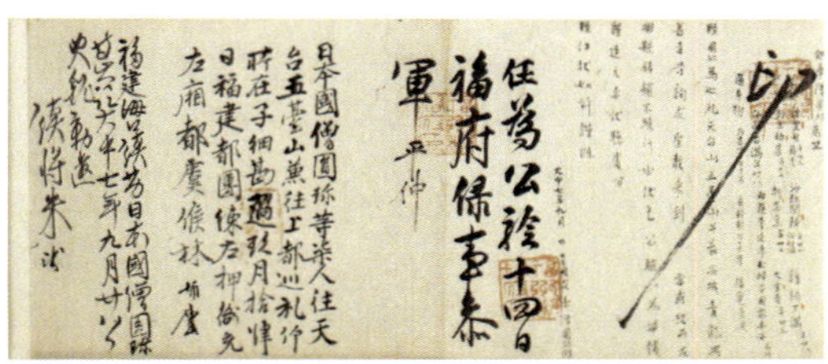

⦿ The second Kugen of Enchin's entry into Tang China

Kugen (i.e. passport and pass). The Kugen issued by Fuzhou kukoshi (provincial governors) for Enchin was eventually taken back to Japan by him. It has been handed down to the present day as a national treasure of Japan and is now collected in Tokyo National Museum. This kugen is believed to be the earliest physical official document in Fujian. It is an important document to understand the local system, inland transportation, and the exit and entry management system of Fujian in the Tang Dynasty.

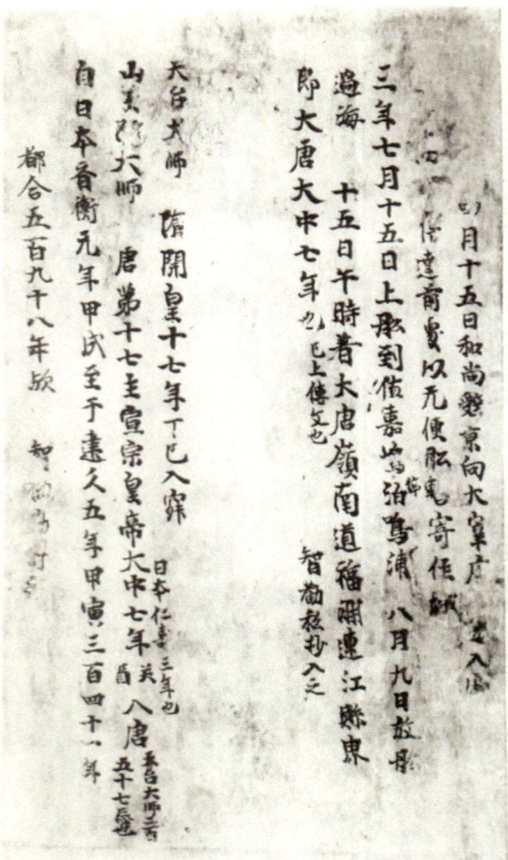

月十五日和尚發京向大宰府
得達前貴以元便船寄住城
三年七月十五日上船到值嘉嶋泊鳴浦　八月九日放船
過海　十五日午時着大唐嶺南道福州連江縣界
即大唐大中七年也　已上傳文也　智慧輪抄入之
天台大師　隋開皇十七年丁巳入寂
山王院大師　唐第十七主宣宗皇帝大中七年癸酉入唐　日本仁壽三年也　天台大師云五十七歲
自日本香衡元年甲戌至于遠久五年甲寅三百四十一年
都合五百九十八年歟

⦿ The Record of the *Pilgrimage* by Enchin, sample page

⦿ The statue of Enchin

3 The Monk Kūkai to Fujian

In 804, the 18th batch of Japanese envoys to Tang Dynasty China came in four ocean-going ships. Among them, Kūkai, the learned monk, Fujiwara no Kadanomaro, the ambassador to the Tang Dynasty China, and Ishikawa Michimasu, the Deputy envoy, came on the first ship. After returning to Japan, Kūkai founded Shingong Buddhism and built the Kongōbu-ji Temple in Mount Kōya. In 921, Kūkai was granted the title of Kōbō Daishi (The Grand Master Who Propagated the Dharma) by the Japanese imperial court. In today's Japan, the Shingong Buddhism Kūkai created has 18 *honzans* (sects) with tens of millions of believers. As a pioneer of Japanese culture, he has earned a high reputation.

⦿ Statue of Kūkai

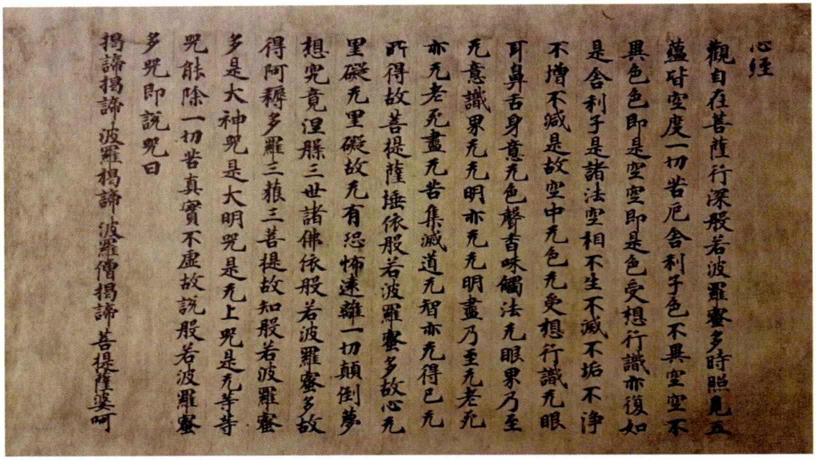

心経
觀自在菩薩行深般若波羅蜜多時照見五
蘊皆空度一切苦厄舍利子色不異空空不
異色色即是空空即是色受想行識亦復如
是舍利子是諸法空相不生不滅不垢不淨
不增不減是故空中无色无受想行識无眼
耳鼻舌身意无色聲香味觸法无眼界乃至
无意識界无无明亦无无明盡乃至无老死
亦无老死盡无苦集滅道无智亦无得已无
所得故菩提薩埵依般若波羅蜜多故心无
罣礙无罣礙故无有恐怖遠離一切顛倒夢
想究竟涅槃三世諸佛依般若波羅蜜多故
得阿耨多羅三藐三菩提故知般若波羅蜜
多是大神咒是大明咒是无上咒是无等等
咒能除一切苦真實不虛故說般若波羅蜜
多咒即說咒曰
揭諦揭諦波羅揭諦波羅僧揭諦菩提薩婆呵

⊙ Manuscript of the *Heart Sutra*, sample page

⊙ A Japanese Shingong pilgrimage group worshiping in front of Memorial Hall of Master Kūkai

⊙ Monument of Kūkai's Arrival (Xiapu Chi'an)

⊙ Crossing the sea to Fujian, China

⊙ Memorial Hall of Master Kūkai

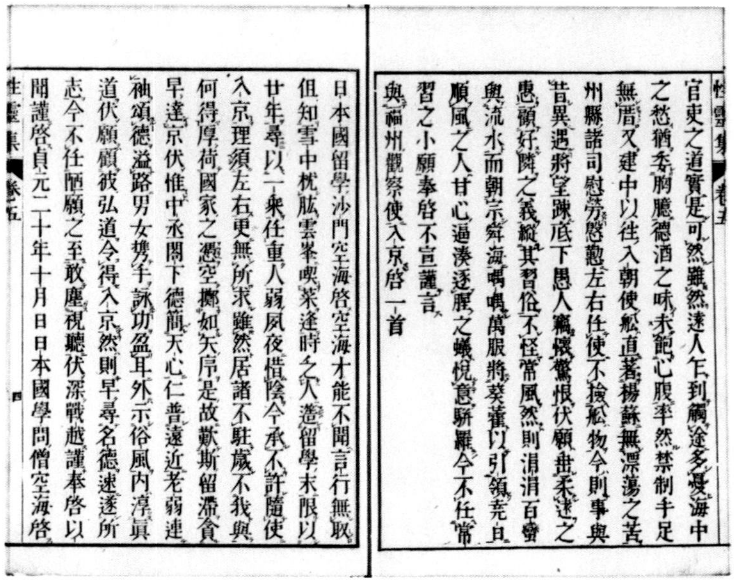
性靈集 卷五

官吏之道實是可然雖然遠人乍到觸途多憂海中之愁猶委胸臆德酒之味未飽心腹率然禁制手足無厝又建中以往入朝使船直著揚蘇無漂蕩之苦州縣諸司慰勞慇懃左右任使不撿船物今則事與昔異遇將望踈底下愚人竊懷驚恨伏願垂柔遠之恵顧好隣之義縱其習俗不怪常風然則涓涓百蠻與流水而朝宗舜海喁喁萬服將葵藿以引領堯日順風之人甘心逼湊逐腥之蟻悅意駢羅今不任常習之小願奉啓不宣謹言

與福州觀察使入京啓一首

日本國留學沙門空海啓空海才能不聞言行無取但知雪中枕肱雲峯喫菜逢時乏人叨留學末限以廿年尋以一乘任重人弱夙夜惜陰今承不許隨使入京理須左右更無所求雖然居諸不駐歳不我與何得厚荷國家之凞空擲如矢之序是故歎斯留滯貪早達京伏惟中丞閣下德簡天心仁普遠近老弱連袂頌德溢路男女携手詠功盈耳外示俗風內淳眞道伏願顧彼弘道令得入京然則早尋名德速遂所志今不任陋願之至敢塵視聽伏深戰越謹奉啓以聞謹啓貞元二十年十月日日本國學問僧空海啓

性靈集 卷五

⦿ *The Letter to Fuzhou Inspector*, sample pages

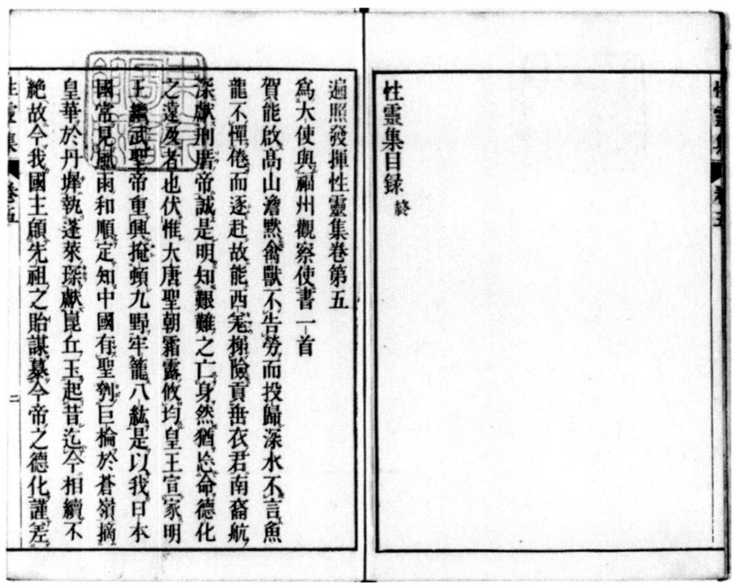
性靈集 卷五

性靈集目録 終

遍照發揮性靈集卷第五

為大使與福州觀察使書一首

賀能啓高山澹默禽獸不告勞而投歸深水不言魚龍不憚倦而逐赴故能西羌梯險貢垂衣君南裔航深獻琛帝誠是明知艱難之亡身然猶忘命德化之遠及者也伏惟大唐聖朝霜露攸均皇王宜家明王繼武聖帝重興掩頓九野牢籠八紘是以我日本國常見風雨和順定知中國有聖刳巨掄於蒼嶺摘皇華於丹墀執蓬萊琛獻崑丘玉起昔迄今相續不絶故今我國主顧先祖之貽謀慕今帝之德化謹差

性靈集 卷五

⦿ *The Letter to Fuzhou Inspector from the Ambassador*, sample pages

⦿ Part of Kongōbu-ji Temple

⦿ Memorial hall of Master Kūkai, Lingyuan Pavilion, Kaiyuan Temple, Fuzhou

信風、第一・第二船同発入海。比及海中、八日初更、風急波高、打破左右棚根、潮水満船、蓋板挙流、人物随漂、無遺夕撮米水。副使小野朝臣石根等卅八人・唐使趙宝英等廿五人、同時没入、不得相救。但臣一人潜行着舳艦角、顧眄前後、生理絶路。十一日五更、帆檣倒於船底、断為両段、舳艫各去未知所到。卌余人累居方丈之舳、挙舳欲没、載纜枕柂、得少浮上、脱却衣裳、裸身懸坐。米水不入口、已経六日、以十三日亥時漂着肥後国天草郡西仲嶋。臣之再生、叡造所救、不任歓幸之至。謹奉表以聞。

【史料3】『日本後紀』延暦二十四年六月乙巳条

遣唐使第一船到泊対馬島下県郡。大使従四位上藤原朝臣葛野麻呂上奏言、臣葛野麻呂等、去年七月六日、発従肥前国松浦郡田浦、四船入海。七日戌刻、第三・四両船、火信不応。出入死生之間、掣曳波濤之上、都卅四箇日、八月十日、到福州長渓県赤岸鎮已南海口。鎮将杜寧・県令胡延沂等相迎、語云、当州刺使柳冕、縁病去任、新除刺史未来、国家大平者。其向州之路、山谷峻隘、担行不穏、因廻船向州。十月三日、到州。新除観察使兼刺史閻済美処分、且奏、且放廿三人入京。十一月三日、臣等発赴上都。此州去京七千五百廿里、星発星宿、晨昏兼行。十二月廿一日、到上都長楽駅。廿三日、内使趙忠、将飛龍家細馬廿三匹迎来、兼持酒脯宣慰、駕即入京城、於外宅安置供給。特有監使高品劉昴、勾当使院。第二船判官菅原朝臣清公等廿七人、去九月

⦿ The records of the Nihon Kōki (an officially commissioned Japanese history text) about the Japanese ambassador Fujiwara no Kadanomaro sailing into Chi'an Town, Changxi County, Fuzhou

4 INGEN FOUNDED ŌBAKU-SHŪ

⦿ Panorama of Huangbo Temple in Fuqing

Ingen's eastward journey to Nagasaki, following Monk Jianzhen, is another feat of the Chinese monks to promote Buddhism in Japan. He created Ōbaku-shū (one of several schools of Zen in Japanese Buddhism), changed the spread pattern of Zen culture in Japan, and introduced the advanced culture and production technology to them, thus driving the development of the local economy and society forward. Japan named the culture that Ingen brought there during this period Ōbaku culture.

⦿ Monastery gate of Huangbo Temple in Fuqing

⦿ Sitting statue of Zen Master Ingen in Ingen Memorial Hall of Huangbo Temple in Fuqing

⦿ Ingen Bridge of Huangbo Temple in Fuqing

⦿ The Buddhist Texts Library of Huangbo Temple in Fuqing

⦿ Mahavira Hall of Huangbo Temple in Fuqing

⦿ Pagoda of Huangbo Temple in Fuqing

⦿ The monument of the gift *Mahāprajñāpāramitā Sutra* in the Buddhist Texts Library of Huangbo Temple in Fuqing

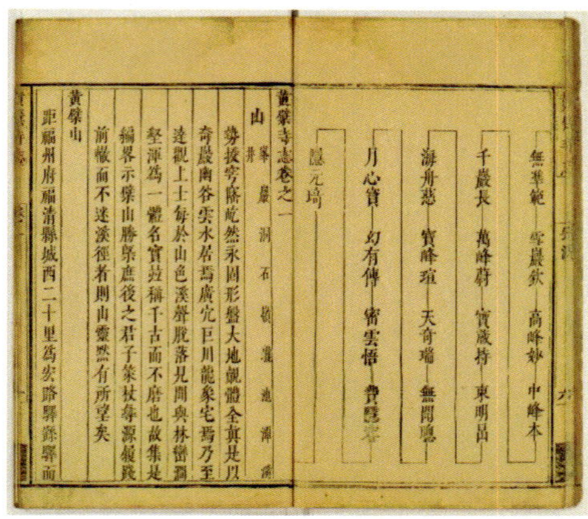

無準範 雪巖欽 高峰妙 中峰本
千巖長 萬峰蔚 寶藏持 東明昂
海舟慈 寶峰瑄 天奇瑞 無聞聰
月心寶 幻有傳 密雲悟 費隱容
隱元琦

黃檗寺志卷之一
山 峯 巖 洞 石 嶺 叢 池 潭 溪 井
勢接穹蒼蔚然永固形盤大地觀體全真是以
奇巖幽谷雲水居焉廣究巨川龍象宅焉乃至
達觀上士每於山色溪聲脫落見聞與林巒渾
堅渾為一體名實並稱千古而不磨也故集是
編畧示檗山勝槩庶後之君子策杖尋源躡跡
前徽而不迷溪徑者則山靈烝有所望矣
黃檗山
距福州府福清縣城西二十里為宏路驛舒驛而

⦿ *Records of Huangbo Temple*, written by Ingen, sample pages

⊙ Ingen Memorial Hall of Huangbo Temple in Fuqing. Built by the donors Yamaoka Yōji and the Yan Mu'e couple, believers of the Ōbaku-shū Sect

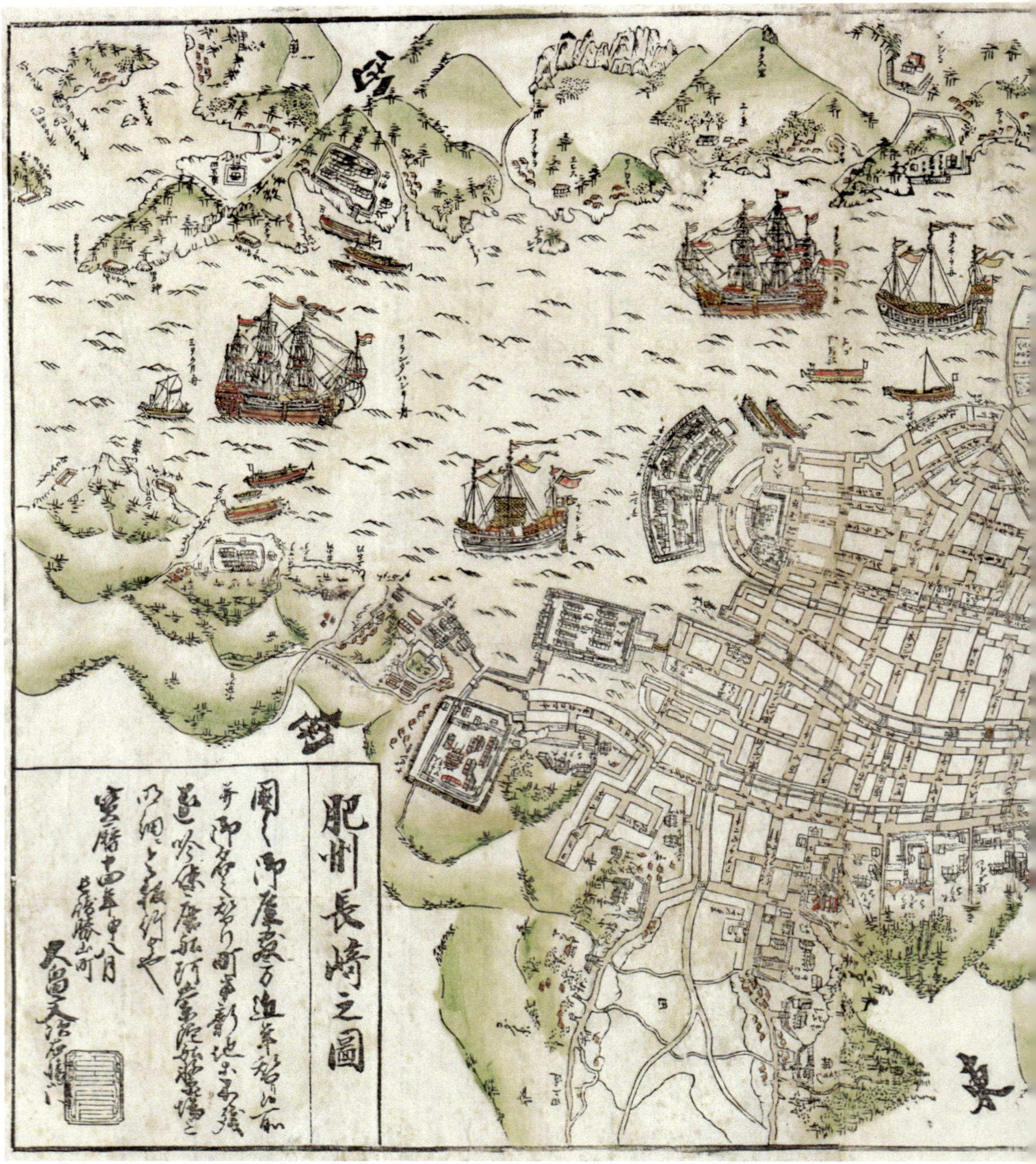

◉ Nagasaki commercial port in the Edo period

⦿ The statue of Itsunen Shoyu, the third generation abbot of Kōfuku-ji temple in Nagasaki, Japan

⦿ Stele of Kōfuku-ji Temple, Nagasaki, Japan. Having arrived in Japan, Ingen lived in this temple and preached the Dharma for one year

The portrait of Ingen, currently collected in Ōbaku-san Manpuku-ji, Kyoto, Japan

Gate of Ōbaku-san Manpuku-ji, Kyoto, Japan

⊙ A distant view of Mahavira Hall of Ōbaku-san Manpuku-ji, Kyoto, Japan

⊙ The temple gate and its inscribed plaque "The First Meaning" of Ōbaku-san Manpuku-ji, Kyoto, Japan

⊙ Mahavira Hall, a significant cultural relic in Japan, of Ōbaku-san Manpuku-ji, Kyoto, Japan

Garan Hall of Ōbaku-san Manpuku-ji, Kyoto, Japan

⦿ Watchman's clapper in the temple

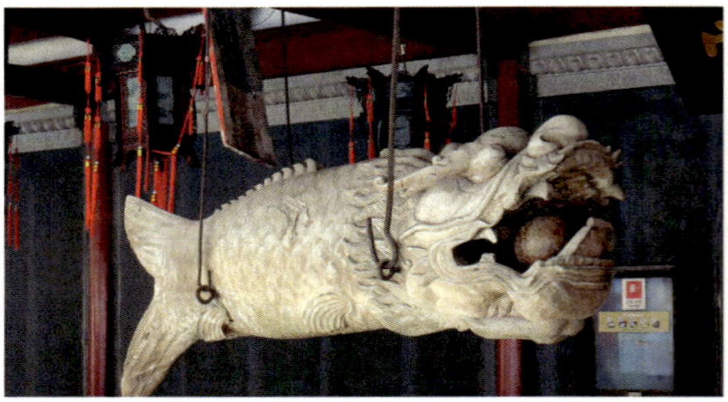

⦿ Watchman's clapper in Yongquan temple, Gushan, Fuzhou

⦿ The woodblock Ingen brought from Fujian for Mahavira Hall. The use of woodblocks in Japanese Buddhist circles began with Ingen.

⦿ Exterior view of the Hall of Four Heavenly Kings of Ōbaku-san Manpuku-ji

⦿ Mahavira Hall, with Fujian architectural style in the Ming Dynasty

◉ Dharma Hall of Ōbaku-san Manpuku-ji

◉ Kaisando Hall of Ōbaku-san Manpuku-ji

⊙ The Memorial Hall of the Founder of Ōbaku-san Manpuku-ji

⊙ Drum-tower of Ōbaku-san Manpuku-ji

⦿ The statue of Mazu of Ōbaku-san Manpuku-ji

⦿ The statue of Vaiśravaṇa of Ōbaku-san Manpuku-ji, by Daosheng Fan, a craftsman from Fujian Province

⦿ The statue of Maitreya of Ōbaku-san Manpuku-ji

The portrait of Garan God (Guan Yu), painted by Daosheng Fan, a craftsman from Fujian Province, and inscribed by Mu'an, collected by Kobe Municipal Museum, Japan

The statue of Skanda of Ōbaku-san Manpuku-ji, by Daosheng Fan, a craftsman from Fujian Province

⦿ In 2011, the board on the outer wall of Ōbaku-san Manpuku-ji was commemorating the 350th anniversary of the founding of Ōbaku-shū

⦿ A hundred gods of Ōbaku-san Manpuku-ji, carved by Daosheng Fan, a craftsman from Fujian Province

⦿ In October 2013, the Dharma meeting of Ōbaku-san Manpuku-ji delivering all creatures from torment was held in Mahavira Hall

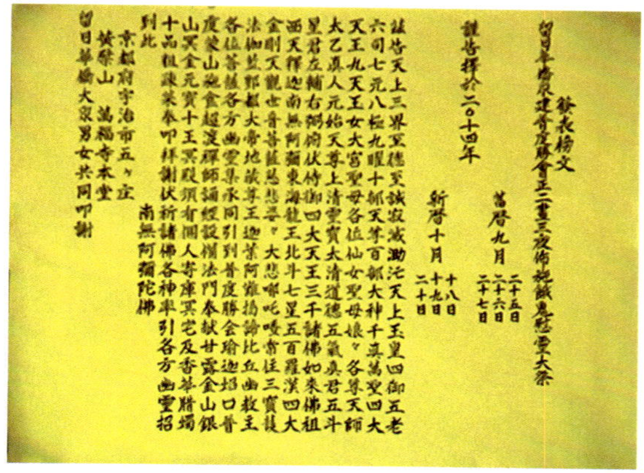

發表榜文
留日華僑京建寺度勝會王二重三夜佈施餓鬼慰靈大祭
舊曆九月 二十五日 二十六日 二十七日
謹告擇於二〇十四年
新曆十月 十八日 十九日 二十日
謹告天上三界眞德眞誠寂滅渺沱天上玉皇四御五老
六司七元八極九曜十部天尊百部大神千眞萬聖四大
天王九天玉女大宮聖母各位仙女聖母娘々各尊天師
太乙眞人元始天尊上清靈寶太清道德五氣眞君五斗
星君左輔右弼斗柄伏持御四大天王三千諸佛如來佛祖
西天釋迦南無阿彌東海龍王北斗七星五百羅漢四大
金剛天觀世音菩薩悲尊〃大悲咖吒嘍帝任三寶護
法伽藍部都大帝地藏尊王迦葉阿難揚論比丘幽救主
各位菩薩各方幽靈集永同引到普度勝會瑜迦招口普
度衆山施食超度禪師誦經設欄法門奉獻甘露金山銀
山冥金元寶十王冥殿須有開人寄庫冥宅及香華賭燭
十品祖隶菜奉叩拜謝状祈請佛各神率引各方幽靈招
到此 南無阿彌陀佛
京都府宇治市五ヶ庄
黄檗山 萬福寺本堂
留日華僑大眾男女共同叩謝

In October 2013, the notice of the Dharma meeting of Ōbaku-san Manpuku-ji delivering all creatures from torment at the Mahavira Hall

In October 2013, the scene of the Dharma meeting of Ōbaku-san Manpuku-ji, delivering all creatures from torment at the Mahavira Hall

Ingen is highly respected in Japan and the emperors of Japan successively granted him a series of titles. His main works are *The Complete Works of Ingen, Monastic Rules for Ōbaku-shū, etc.* These are valuable materials for us to study the history of overseas exchange of Chinese Buddhism.

Ingen was erudite and versatile. In addition to his proficiency in Buddhism, he excelled at medicine, poetry, and especially calligraphy. While preaching the Dharma, he also introduced Chinese vegetarian recipes, and cooking skills to Japan, such as Ingen beans (lentils and kidney beans) commonly seen at a Japanese meal, watermelon, lotus seed, and bamboo shoots, as well as the ornamental plant Moso bamboo. In the Ming Dynasty, the common vegetarian dishes in temples in Fujian and Zhejiang areas were spread by monks in Huangbo mountain to Japan, thus forming the famous Fucha cuisine in Kyoto.

In addition, the monks introduced the popular method of tea frying and drinking to Japan, which formed an important part of Japanese tea culture. These communications greatly enriched Japanese food culture.

⦿ Moso bamboo, which was brought to Japan by Ingen from Fujian, is located in the courtyard of Ōbaku-san Manpuku-ji Temple.

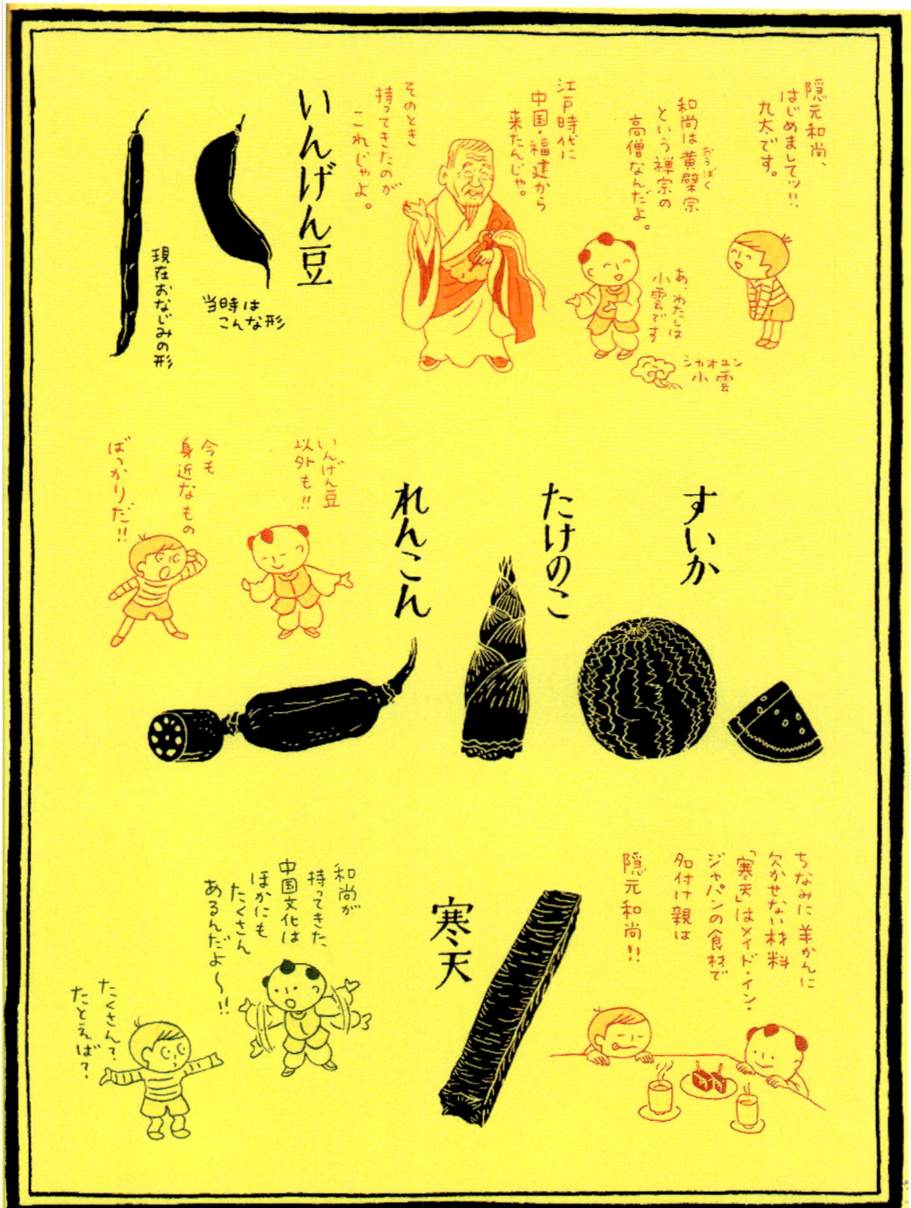

⦿ The depiction of Chinese culture spread by Ingen in Japanese children's books

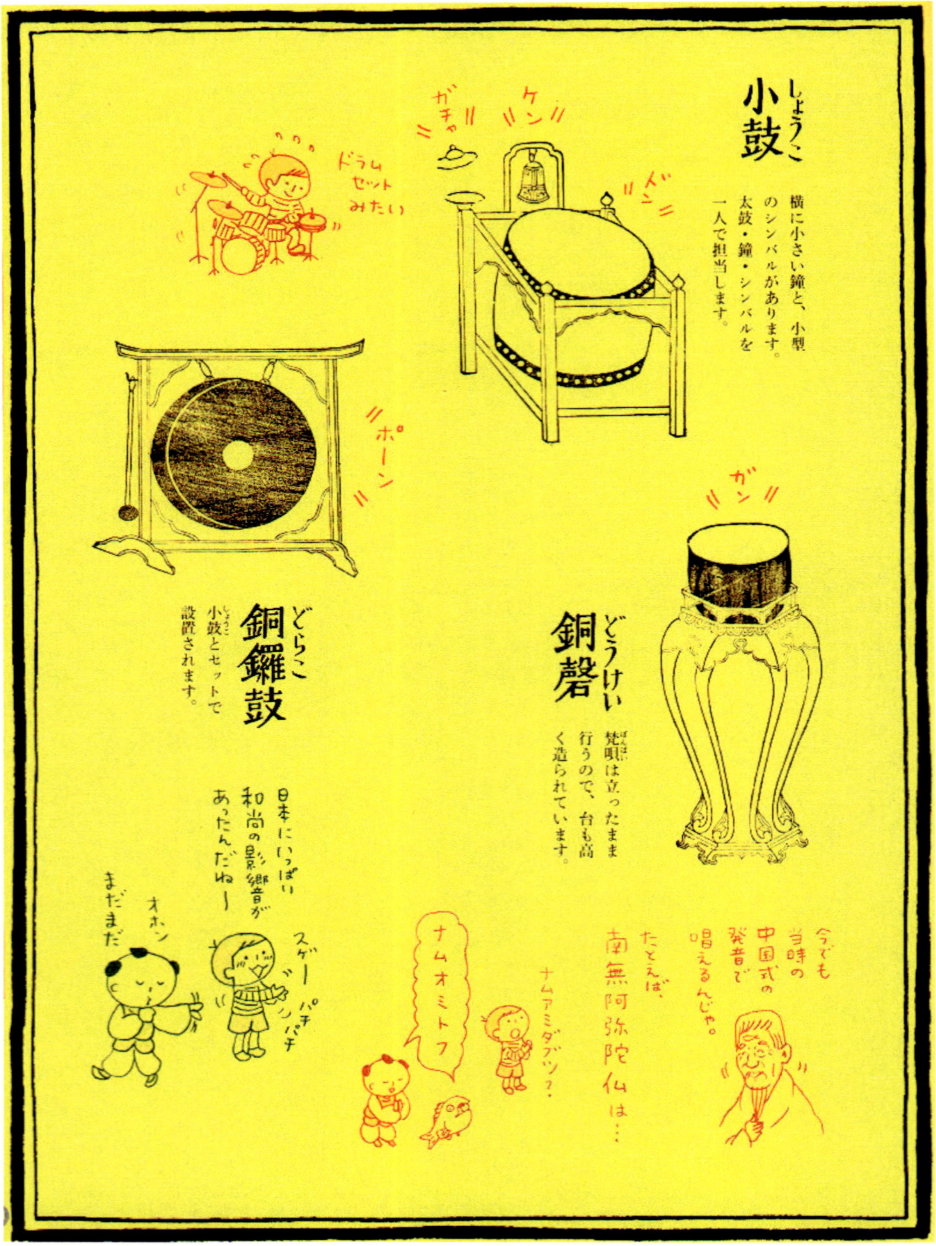

⊙ The depiction of Chinese culture spread by Ingen in Japanese children's books

5 Shilla monks travelling to Fujian

In the Tang Dynasty, there were personnel exchanges between Fujian and Shilla on the Korean Peninsula. As per the *Biography of Tang Eminent Monks Seeking Dharma in the West*, Hyeryun, a monk of the Shilla, came to Fuzhou by sea during the Zhenguan period (627–649) of Emperor Taizong of the Tang Dynasty and went to Chang'an along the state highway to practice Dharma.

⦿ The records of Hyeryun, a Shilla Buddhist monk, who came to Fujian in the Zhenguan period (627–649) of the Tang Dynasty

The records of Honggyeong, a Shilla monk, returning from Fujian of Tang in *History of Goryeo*

During the Tianyou period (904–907) of the Tang Dynasty, Wang Yanbin served as the governor of Quanzhou. He once sought advice from Hyŏnnul, a Korean monk who was preaching Dharma in Quanzhou.

In the Five Dynasties period, Shilla monks kept travelling between the Korean Peninsula and Fujian.

At the end of the Tang Dynasty, a Shilla monk named Gwisan was learning the Dharma from Master Huileng of the Changqing Temple in Fuzhou.

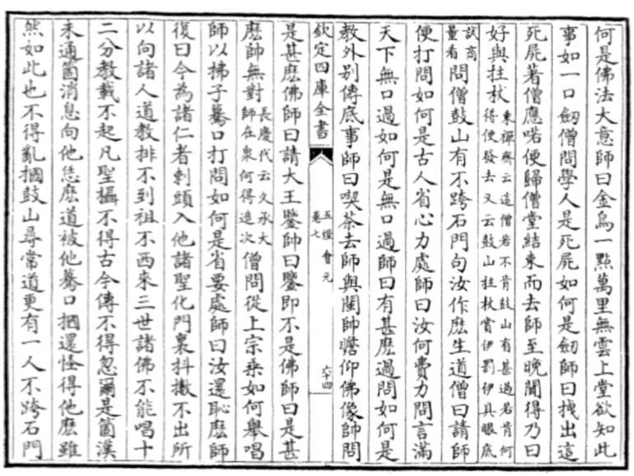

The records of a Zen master's visit to Fujian in *Five-Lantern Festival*

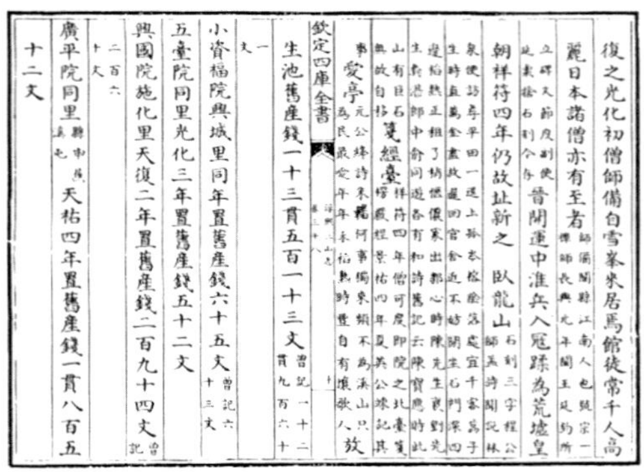

Records of Three Mountains, sample pages

6 Friendships between Chinese and Japanese Buddism

6.1 Friendships between Chinese and Japanese Buddhists

With the prosperity of maritime trade, Buddhism was spreading. A great many Fujian monks came to Japan to promote Buddhism. Thus, Buddhist temples there were built one by one. In Nagasaki, Kyoto, and Nara, there were Buddhist temples with Fujian monks and abbots.

Some Buddhist temples in Japan were funded by Chinese maritime merchants, who used to believe in Buddhism. Their strong economic strength allowed them to undertake the financing of building temples.

(1) Sūfuku-ji Temple

In the sixth year of Kan'ei of Emperor Go-Mizunoo (1629), Sūfuku-ji Temple was built by the "Fuzhou Gang," some Chinese living in Nagasaki. The locals commonly call it "Fuzhou Temple."

⦿ First Peak Gate (founded in 1644)

⦿ Sitting statue of Sakyamuni in the Mahavira Hall

⦿ Sūfuku-ji Temple gate, Nagasaki, Japan

⦿ Vault of the veranda of Mahavira Hall

⦿ Mahavira Hall (founded in 1646)

The architectural layout of Sūfuku-ji Temple in Nagasaki is relatively complete. And the architecture adopted the traditional Chinese Garan shape. It is the oldest existing traditional Buddhist temple in Japan.

⊙ Mazu gate outside Mazu Hall

⊙ Decoration of ogre-shaped tiles on the roof of Mazu gate

⊙ Shengshou Mountain inscribed on the plaque of the temple gate (By Ingen)

(2) Fukusai-ji Temple

Fukusai-ji Temple is located in Chikugomachi in Nagasaki, commonly known as "Quanzhou Temple" or "Zhangzhou Temple." It was founded by the overseas Chinese living in Zhangzhou and Quanzhou in Fujian Province.

⦿ Site model, collected by Nagasaki Historical Archive

⦿ Inscriptions in front of the new site

⦿ The old components in the new site of Fukusai-ji Temple in Nagasaki, Japan

⦿ New site

⦿ Giant turtle and Guanyin statue in the new architecture

⦿ Interior of new main hall

(3) Kōfuku-ji Temple

Kōfuku-ji Temple in Nagasaki is the earliest temple among the four Tang temples in Nagasaki. It was built in 1624 by Zhen'en, a Jiangxi monk who went to Japan in the late Ming Dynasty, with the enthusiastic support of many overseas Chinese business people / believers. Many of them were business people and immigrants from Jiangsu, Zhejiang, and Jiangxi Provinces, and most went to Japan for business on commercial ships sailing from Nanjing. So, the local people call it Nanjing Temple.

⦿ "New to the Holy Land," inscribed on the plaque on the inside of the main beam of the temple gate (By Ingen)

⦿ The windows with ice crack patterns on the side walls of the Mahavira Hall, common in ancient buildings in Fujian

⦿ Kōfuku-ji Temple Gate, Nagasaki, Japan

⦿ The door of the old Chinatown was decorated with Fujian broad leaved fir

⦿ Mazu Hall

⦿ Mahavira Hall (inscribed by Ingen)

6.2 Travel-stained monks

The construction of Huangbo Temple marks the formal establishment of Ōbaku-shū sect in Japan, in addition to Linji school and Caodong school. Thanks to the efforts of Ingen and his disciples, Ōbaku-shū developed rapidly and gradually blended into the Japanese Buddhist community and society. There were over 30 disciples who traveled to Japan with Ingen. Some of them returned home while the rest stayed in Japan promoting the Dharma for life. The famous disciples who stayed in Japan were Damei, Huilin, Duyan, Duzhan, Duhou, Nanyuan, and Daoshi. After that, Mu'an and Sokuhi Nyoitsu from Fujian joined them.

(1) Mu'an Xingtao

Mu'an (1611–1684), surnamed Wu, a native of Jinjiang, Quanzhou, has earned a high status in Japanese Zen circles. He had over 50 disciples, most of whom were Japanese.

⦿ The portrait of Mu'an, collected by Kobe Municipal Museum, Japan

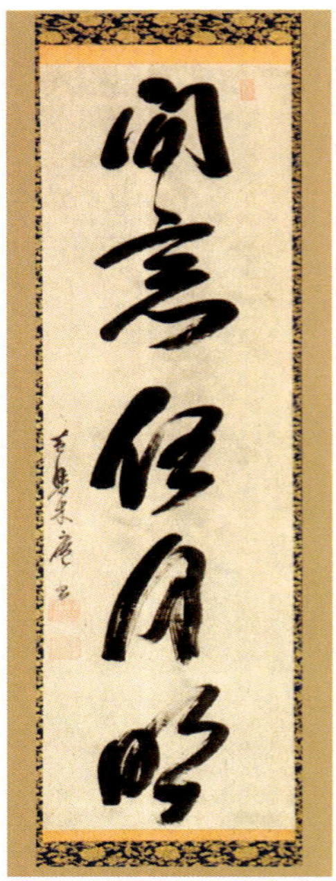

⦿ Treasured scrolls of calligraphy, collected by the Indianapolis Museum of Art, USA

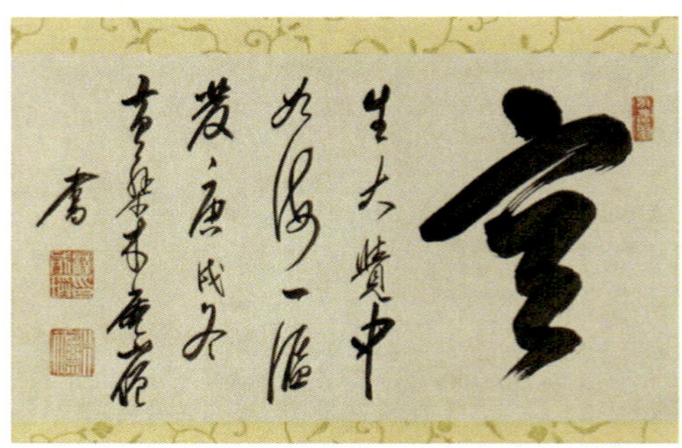

⦿ Treasured scrolls of calligraphy, collected by the Museum of Asian Art, San Francisco, USA

(2) Sokuhi Nyoitsu

Sokuhi Nyoitsu (1616–1671) was born in Fuqing, Fuzhou. At the age of 18, he became a monk. He first learned from eminent monks, such as Miyun, Feiyin, and Yongjue, before becoming a disciple of Ingen.

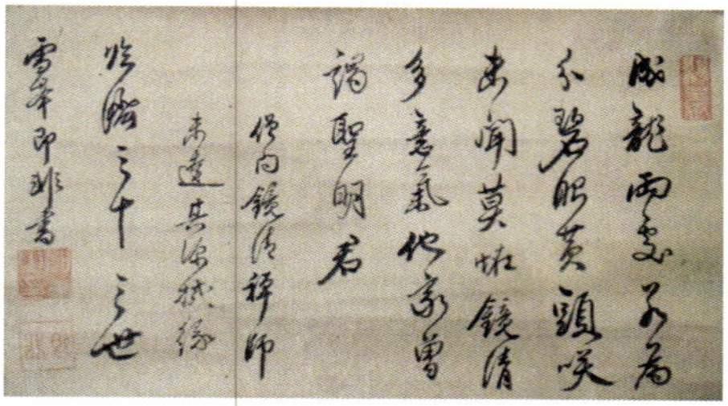

⦿ Treasured scrolls of calligraphy

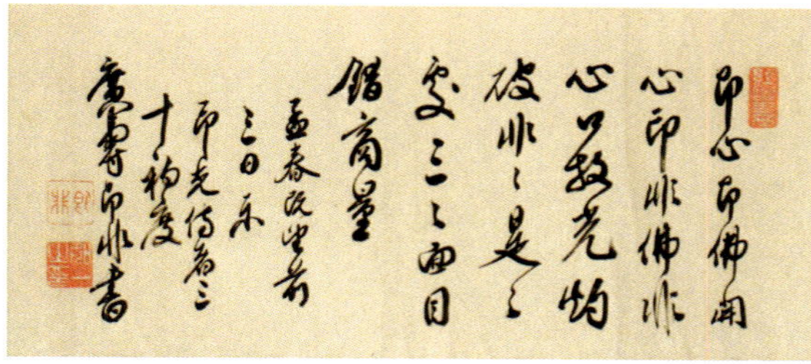

⦿ Treasured scrolls of calligraphy, collected by the Philadelphia Museum of Art, USA

⦿ Self-inscribed self-portrait of Sokuhi Nyoitsu

⦿ The portrait of Sokuhi Nyoitsu and Sengai Shōan, master and disciple

(3) Huilin Xingji

Huilin (1609–1681), commonly known as Zheng Xingzhi, became a monk at the age of 40. He was from Fuqing, Fuzhou. As a disciple of Ingen, he stayed in Japan for 27 years. He wrote *Quotations of Erhui, The Sound of Waves*, etc.

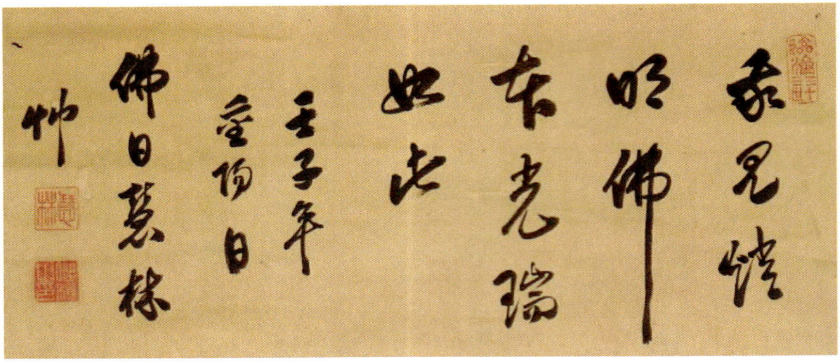

⦿ Treasured scrolls of calligraphy by Huilin

(4) Duzhan Xingying

Duzhan (1628–1706), a native of Putian, Fujian Province, has a common surname of Chen. He stayed in Japan for 52 years. His works *include Quotations, The Life of Buddhist Monks in Fusang, Praise of Pure Land, Pure Land Poetry, Painting of Blessing and Chanting Buddha, Origin of Taima Mandala*, etc.

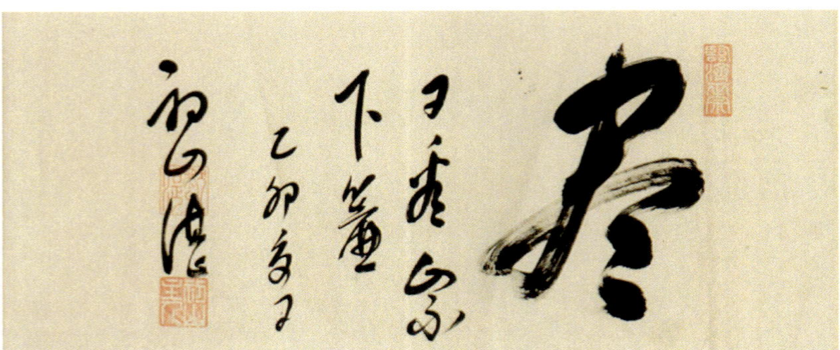

⦿ Treasured scrolls of calligraphy by Duzhan, collected by the Philadelphia Museum of Art, USA

(5) Nanyuan Xingpai

Nanyuan (1631–1692), with the common surname of Lin, was born in Fuqing, Fuzhou. He spent 29 years in Japan. The works of Nanyuan are *Records of Antiques* (30 volumes), *Zhilin Collection* (24 volumes), *Zanglin Collection* (1 volume), etc.

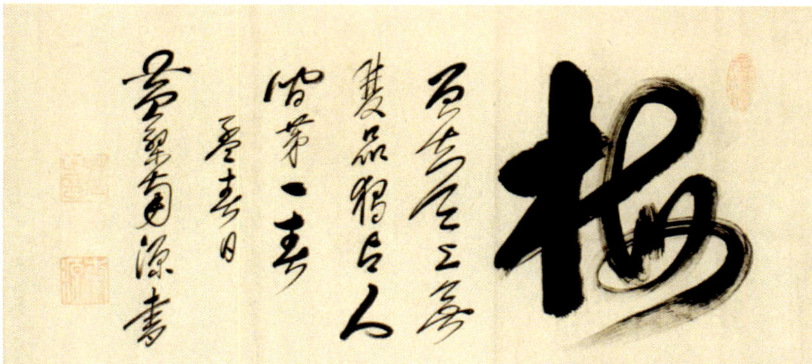

⦿ Treasured scrolls of calligraphy by Duzhan, collected by the Philadelphia Museum of Art, USA

(6) Duhou Xingshi

Duhou (1624–1688), a native of Fuzhou, has a common surname of Zhu and a nickname of Xiufeng. He stayed in Japan for 34 years. He wrote *The Five-cloud Collection* (4 volumes).

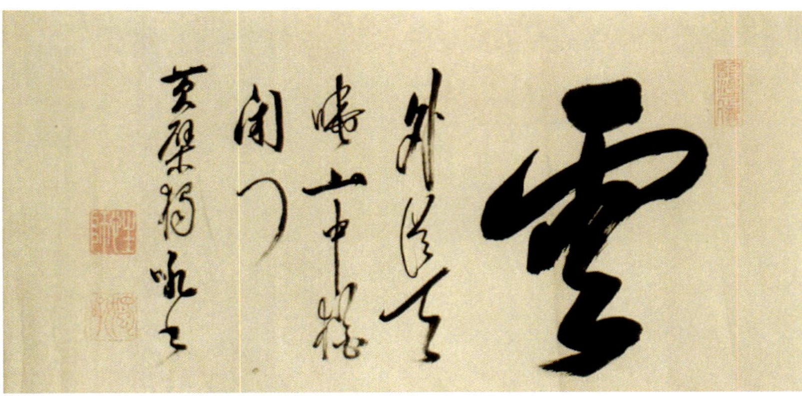

⦿ Treasured scrolls of calligraphy by Duhou, collected by the Philadelphia Museum of art, USA

(7) Gaoquan Xingdun

Gaoquan (1633–1695), with a common surname of Lin and first name of Liangwei, was a Taoist of Tanhua and native of Fuqing in Fuzhou. His works were the *Biography of Buddhist Monks in Fusang* (10 volumes), *Sequel of Biography of Buddhist Monks in Fusang* (3 volumes), *Biography of Eminent Monks in Japan* (10 volumes), and more.

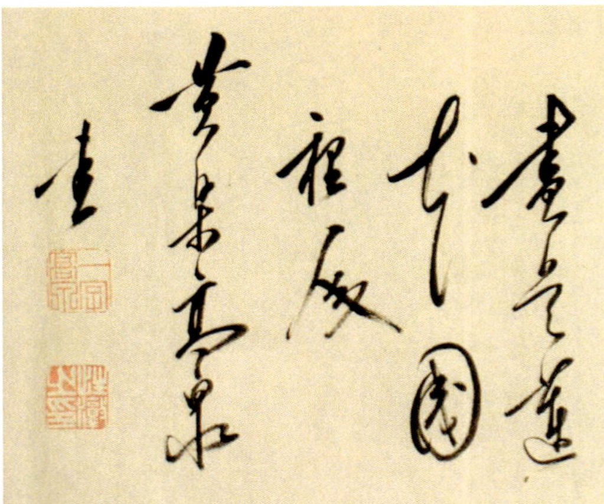

⦿ Treasured scroll of calligraphy by Gaoquan, collected by the Philadelphia Museum of Art, USA

⦿ Treasured scrolls of calligraphy by Gaoquan, collected by the Jiangsu Antique Gallery

(8) Sengai Shōan

Sengai Shōan (1636–1705) was a native of Changle District, Fuzhou City, with the common surname of Chen, a Buddhist name of Shōan, and a Taoist name of Sengai. He traveled to Japan with his master in 1657. He died at the age of 70 and excelled at calligraphy.

⦿ Fushimi Shakubu-ji Temple, Kyoto, Japan

⦿ Portrait of Sengai Shōan

(9) Yueshan Daozong

Yueshan (1629–1709) was a native of Quanzhou, Fujian, with the common surname of Sun. He arrived in Japan in 1657 at the age of 29. He was adept at Japanese calligraphy, and thus was given the name Calligrapher Yueshan by the Japanese.

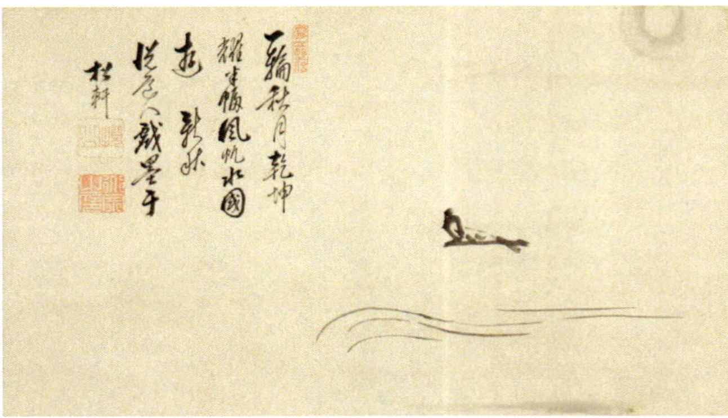

⦿ Treasured scrolls of calligraphy by Yueshan, collected by the Minamiyamate Art Gallery, Nagasaki, Japan

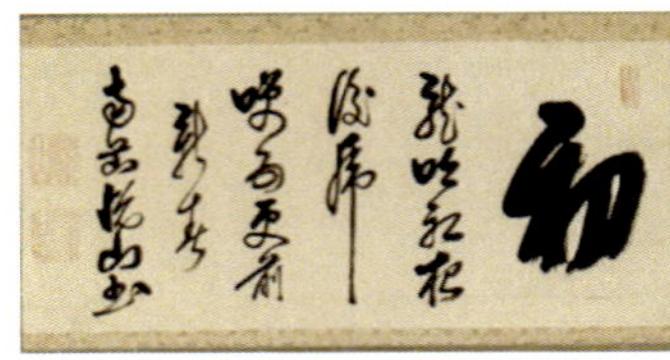

⦿ Treasured scrolls of calligraphy by Yueshan, collected by the Cleveland Museum of Art, USA

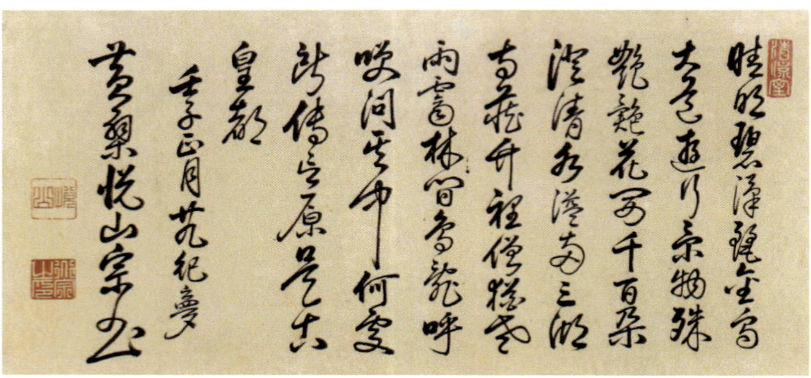

⦿ Treasured scrolls of calligraphy by Yueshan, collected by the Minamiyamate Art Gallery, Nagasaki, Japan

CHAPTER 3

THE CONSTRUCTION OF NORTHEAST ASIA BUSINESS DISTRICT BY THE FUJIANESE

The advancement of navigation technology and the development of the social economy have enabled Fujian maritime merchants to set foot in the East and the West. The mutual trade between them and those from Northeast Asian countries has contributed to a close relationship between Fujian and these regions, thus the economic development and cultural exchanges among Northeast Asian regions.

1 Ships Coming from the South

During this period, Fuzhou port had received a considerable number of trade vessels, a prosperous scene of trade when the vessels gathered.

In the Northern Song Dynasty, Fujian maritime merchants often sailed to Japan for trade. In 1002, Zhou Shichang, a maritime merchant from Fujian Province, and his merchant ships were taken to Japan by storm. Well-received by the Japanese Imperial Court, he stayed in Japan for seven years. During his stay, Zhou and Japanese poets exchanged poems. When he decided to return home, Fujiki Yoshi and Zhou sailed together to Song Dynasty China. Emperor Zhenzong of the Song Dynasty personally received Fujiki Yoshi, presented him with fashionable clothing, and copper coins, and had him escorted back to Japan.

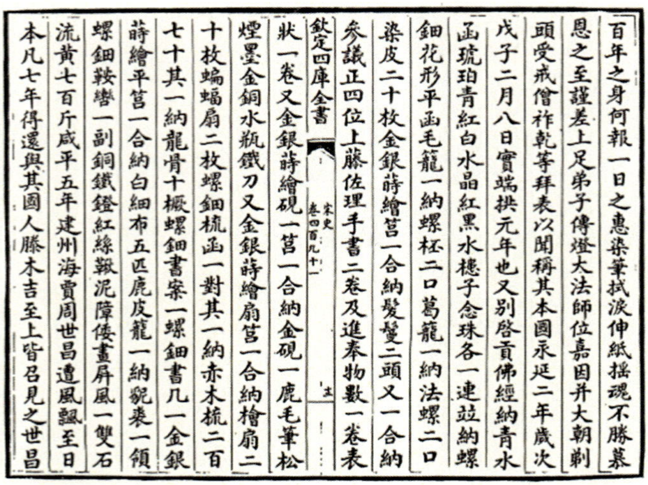

百年之身何報一日之惠染筆拭淚伸紙揺魂不勝慕
恩之至謹差上足弟子傳燈大法師位嘉因幷大朝剃
頭受戒僧祚乾等拜表以聞稱其本國永延二年歳次
戊子二月八日實端拱元年也又別啓貢佛經納青木
函琥珀青紅白水晶紅黑木槵子念珠各一連並納螺
鈿花形平函毛籠一納螺杯二口葛籠一納法螺二口
染皮二十枚金銀蒔繪筥一合納髮鬘二頭又一合納
參議正四位上藤佐理手書二卷及進奉物數一卷表
欽定四庫全書 宋史 卷四百九十一
狀一卷又金銀蒔繪硯一筥一合納金硯一鹿毛筆松
煙墨金銅水瓶鐵刀又金銀蒔繪扇筥一合納檜扇二
十枚蝙蝠扇二枚螺鈿梳函一對其一納赤木梳二百
七十其一納龍骨十橛螺鈿書案一螺鈿書几一金銀
蒔繪平筥一合納白細布五匹鹿皮籠一納貂裘一領
螺鈿鞍轡一副銅鐵鐙紅絲鞦泥障倭畫屏風一雙石
流黃七百斤咸平五年建州海賈周世昌遭風飄至日
本凡七年得還與其國人滕木吉至上皆召見之世昌

The Records of Zhou Shichang, a maritime merchant in Jianzhou, who returned from Japan and Fujiki Yoshi, a Japanese, who accompanied his return in the *History of the Song Dynasty*

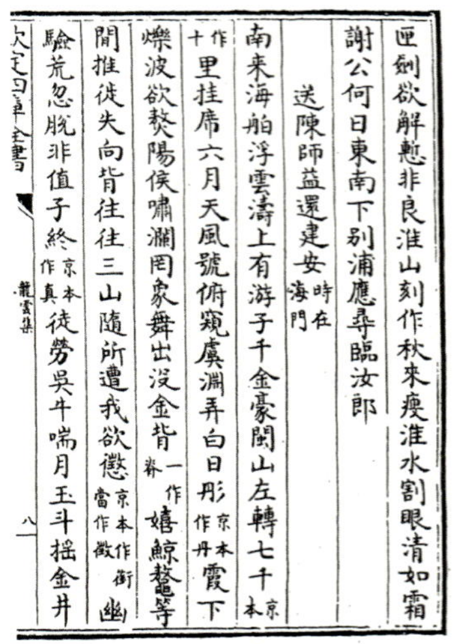

匣劍欲解慙非良淮山刻作秋來瘦淮水割眼清如霜
謝公何日東南下別浦應尋臨汝郎
送陳師益還建安 時在海門
南來海舶浮雲濤上有游子千金豪閩山左轉七千 京本作十
里挂席六月天風號俯窺虞淵弄白日彤 京本作丹 霞下
爍波欲焚陽侯嘯淵罔象舞出沒金背 一作脊 嬉鯨鼇等
閒推徙失向背往往三山隨所遭我欲徵 京本作徵當作微 幽
驗荒忽朓非值子終 京本作真 徒勞吳牛喘月玉斗揺金井
欽定四庫全書 龍雲集

Send Chen Shiyi Back to Jian'an, by Liu Yan of the Song Dynasty, sample page

In the autumn of 1026, Chen Wenyou, a businessman from Fuzhou, returned from Japan. In the next year (1027), he sailed again to Japan. In September of 1028, Zhou Wenyi, a Fuzhou businessman who lived in Taizhou, sailed to Japan for business for the second time. In December, he wrote to Fujiwara no Sanesuke, *udaijin* (Minister of the Right), and gifted him with local products, including an emerald-patterned brocade, a little patterned silk brocade, a big patterned white silk, musk, clove, aloes, and various kinds of stationaries.

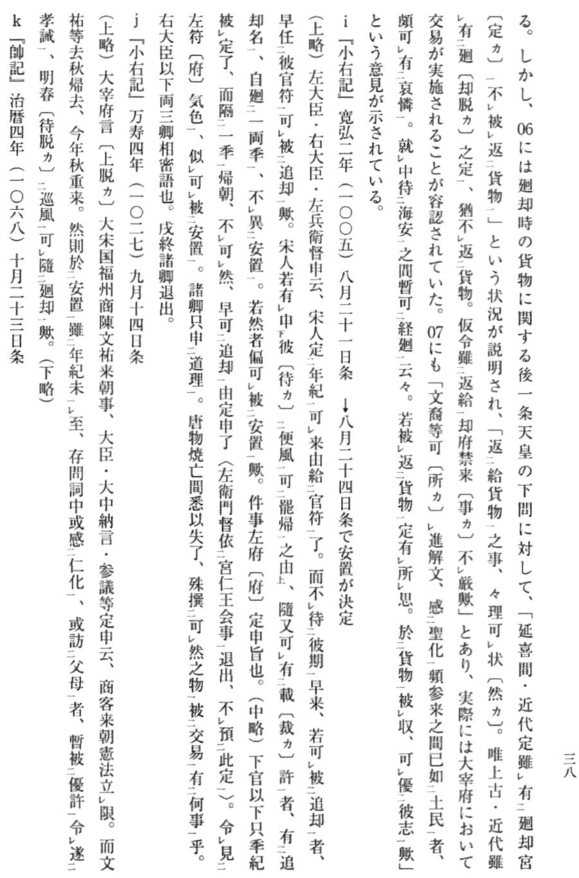

三八

る。しかし、06には廻却時の貨物に関する後一条天皇の下問に対して、「延喜間・近代定雖有廻却宮〔定カ〕不被返貨物」という状況が説明され、「返給貨物之事、々理可状〔然カ〕。唯上古・近代雖有廻〔却脱カ〕之定、猶不返貨物。仮令雖返給却府禁来〔事カ〕不厳歟」とあり、実際には大宰府において交易が実施されることが容認されていた。07にも「文裔等可〔所カ〕進解文、感聖化頻参来之間已如土民者、頗可有哀憐。就中待海安之間暫可経廻云々。若被返貨物定有所思。於貨物被収、可優彼志歟」という意見が示されている。

i 『小右記』寛弘二年（一〇〇五）八月二十一日条 ↓八月二十四日条で安置が決定

（上略）左大臣・右大臣・左兵衛督申云、宋人定年紀可来由給官符了。而不待彼期早来、若可被追却者、早任彼官符可被追却歟。宋人若有申彼〔待カ〕便風可罷帰之由、随又可有栽〔裁カ〕許者、有追却名、自廻一両季、不異安置。若然者偏可被安置歟。件事左府〔府〕定申旨也。（中略）下官以下只季紀被定了、而隔一季帰朝、不可然、早可追却由定申了〈左衛門督依宮仁王会事退出、不預此定〉。令見左符〔府〕気色、似可被安置。諸卿只申道理。唐物焼亡間悉以失了、殊撰可然之物被交易有何事乎。右大臣以下両三卿相密語也。戌終諸卿退出。

j 『小右記』万寿四年（一〇二七）九月十四日条

（上略）大宰府言〔上脱カ〕大宋国福州商陳文祐来朝事、大臣・大中納言・参議等定申云、商客来朝憲法立限。而文祐等去秋帰去、今年秋重来。然則於安置雖年紀未至、存問詞中或感仁化、或訪父母者、暫被優許令遂孝誠、明春〔待脱カ〕巡風可随廻却歟。（下略）

k 『帥記』治暦四年（一〇六八）十月二十三日条

⊙ The Records of Chen Wenyou, a merchant from Fuzhou, engaged in business in Japan in the ancient Japanese literature *Shōyūki*, sample page

In 1068, Pan Huaiqing, a businessman from Fuzhou, went to Japan for trade. In 1070, He made another trip there and offered Buddha statues to *Dazaifu* (a Japanese term for the regional government in Kyushu from the 8th to the 12th centuries). In 1072, Jōjin, a Japanese monk, boarded a Tang ship to Song China to seek the Dharma from Matsuura of Hizen Province (now Higashimatsuura of Saga Prefecture). There were three other passengers onboard: Zeng Ju from Nanxiong, Wu Zhu from Fuzhou, and Zheng Qing from Quanzhou. Emperor Shenzong of the Song Dynasty received Jōjin and inquired him what kind of Chinese goods the Japanese needed. He answered fragrant medicine, tea bowls, brocade, and sappan wood.

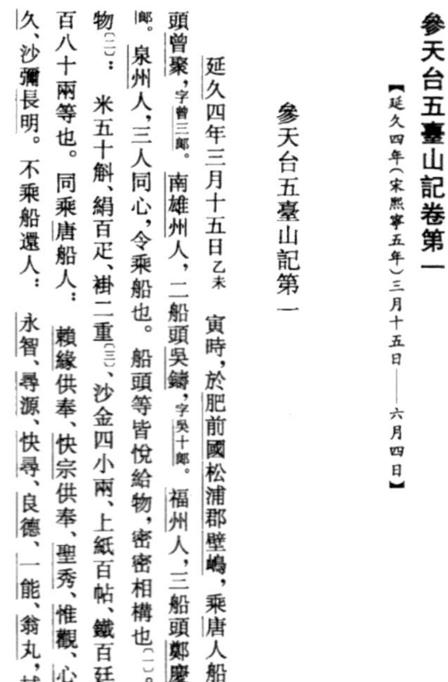

參天台五臺山記卷第一

【延久四年（宋熙寧五年）三月十五日——六月四日】

參天台五臺山記第一

延久四年三月十五日乙未 寅時，於肥前國松浦郡壁嶋，乘唐人船，一船頭曾聚，字曾三郎。南雄州人，二船頭吳鑄，字吳十郎。福州人，三船頭鄭慶，字鄭三郎。泉州人，三人同心，令乘船也。船頭等皆悅給物，密密相構也(一)。志與物(二)：米五十斛、絹百疋、褂二重(三)、沙金四小兩、上紙百帖、鐵百廷、水銀百八十兩等也。同乘唐船人：賴緣供奉、快宗供奉、聖秀、惟觀、心賢、善久、沙彌長明。不乘船還人：永智、尋源、快尋、良德、一能、翁丸，拭淚離

卷第一　一

⦿ The records of Japanese monks taking the Tang Dynasty ships to seek Dharma in China in *San Tendai Godai San Ki*

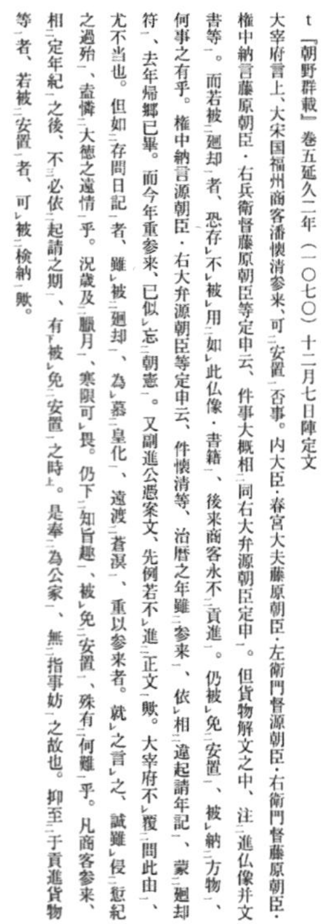

『朝野群載』卷五延久二年（一〇七〇）十二月七日陣定文

大宰府言上、大宋国福州商客潘懐清参来、可安置否事。内大臣・春宮大夫藤原朝臣・左衛門督源朝臣・右衛門督藤原朝臣・権中納言藤原朝臣・右兵衛督藤原朝臣等定申云、件事大概相同右大弁源朝臣定申。但貨物解文之中、注進仏像并文書等。而若被廻却者、恐存不被用如此仏像・書籍、後来商客永不貢進。仍被免安置、被納方物、何事之有乎。権中納言源朝臣・右大弁源朝臣等定申云、件懐清等、治暦之年雖参来、依相違起請年記、蒙廻却符、去年帰郷已畢。而今年重参来、已似忘朝憲。又副進公憑案文、先例若不進正文歟。大宰府不覆問此由、尤不当也。但如存問日記者、雖被廻却、為慕皇化、遠渡蒼溟、重以参来者。就之言之、誠難侵愆紀之過殆、盍憐大徳之遠情乎。況歳及臘月、寒限可畏。仍下知旨趣、被免安置、殊有何難乎。凡商客参来、相定年紀之後、不必依起請之期、有被免安置之時。是奉為公家、無指事妨之故也。抑至于貢進貨物等者、若被安置者、可被検納歟。

⦿ A study of Fuzhou merchants in the Japanese *Chōyagunsai*, records of Pan Huaiqing's trade with Japan

From 1102 to 1105, Li Chong, a Quanzhou merchant, twice travelled to Hakatanotsu, Japan to engage in trade. On his second visit to Dazaifu, he submitted an official certificate issued by the Bureau of Foreign Shipping of Song Dynasty China to request permission to trade. This certificate is the complete foreign trade certificate of the Song Dynasty, which is valuable information for us to understand the foreign shipping system, import and export, and Fujian maritime shipping organization in the Song Dynasty.

中国帆船による東アジア海域交流（松浦）

1080	承暦四年	閏8	宋商	孫　忠③	明州よりの牒状
1080	承暦四年	9	宋商	黄　逢	
1080	承暦四年	10	宋商		
1080	承暦四年	9	宋商	劉勝參	
1081	永保元年		宋商	劉　昆①	
1082	永保二年	8	宋商	楊　有	
1082	永保二年	8	宋商	孫　忠①	
1082	永保二年	9	宋商	劉　昆①	
1085	應徳二年	7	宋商		
1085	應徳二年	10	宋商	孫　忠②	
1085	應徳二年	10	宋商	林　皐	
1091	寛治五年	7	宋商	堯　忠	
1091	寛治五年	8	宋商	季居簡	
1092	寛治六年	6	宋商	劉　昆②	契丹経由
1093	寛治七年	4	宋商客	林　通	福州商客
1102	康和四年		宋商客	李　充①	泉州商客
1104	長治元年		宋商客	李　充②	泉州商客
1105	長治二年	8	宋商客	李　充③	泉州商客
1110	天永元年	4	宋商	李　先	
1118	元永元年	2	宋商	陳次明	
1127	大治二年	12	宋商		
1128	大治三年	8	宋商	曾周意	
1133	長承二年	8	宋商	周　新	
1148	久安四年		宋商		
1150	久安六年		宋商	劉文仲①	
1151	仁平元年	9	宋商	劉文仲②	
1169	嘉應元年		宋綱首		文献通考
1179	治承三年	2			新渡・太平御覧
1180	治承四年	10	宋商船		摂津輪田泊に入港
1191	建久二年		宋綱首	楊三綱	栄西帰朝
1218	建保六年		宋綱首	張光安	
1254	建長六年	4			唐船数五艘と定める

出典：森克己「日・宋・麗交通貿易年表」（『新訂日宋貿易の研究』森克己著作選集第1巻、国書刊行会、1975年）、528-564頁

上表に見える康和四年（1102）、長治元年（1104）、長治二年（1105）と連続して日本に来航した李充に関して、『朝野群載』巻二十、異国の条に見える「同存問記」によれば、

長治二年八月二十二日、存問大宋國客記

問客云。警固所去二十日解狀稱、今日酉時、大宋國船壹艘、到来筑前國那珂郡博多津志賀島前海。……客申云。先來大宋國、泉州人李充也。充去康和四年爲莊厳之人徒、參來貴朝。……[1)]

とあるように、泉州の海商李充が日本の博多の志賀島に来航している。彼の最初の来航は康和四年（1102）であり、その時は荘厳の船に搭乗しての日本来航であった。この時の日本への来航時に宋の官憲から給

1）国史大系本『朝野群載』吉川弘文館、1964年、451頁

⦿ The records of Li Chong, a Quanzhou businessman in the Song Dynasty, visiting Japan in the article of Japanese scholar Akira Matsuura

倭國
倭國在泉之東北今號日本國以其國近日出故名或
曰惡舊名改之國方數千里西南至海東北限以大山
山外即毛人國凡五畿七道三島三千七百七十二鄉
四百一十四驛八十八萬三千餘丁地多山林無良田
嗜海錯俗多文身自謂泰伯之後又言上古使至中國
皆自稱大夫昔夏少康之子封於會稽斷髮文身以避
蛟龍之害今倭人沈沒取魚亦文身以厭水族計其道
里在會稽之正東氣候大類中國王以王爲姓歷七十
餘世不易文武皆世官男子衣橫幅結束相連不施縫
婦人衣如單被穿其中以貫頭一衣率用二三縑皆
諸蕃志卷上
照曠閣

被髮跣足亦有中國典籍如五經白樂天文集之類皆
自中國得之土宜五穀而少麥交易用銅錢以乾文大
寶爲文有水牛驢羊犀象之屬亦有金銀細絹花布多
產杉木羅木長至十四五丈徑四尺餘土人解爲枋板
以巨艦搬運至吾泉貿易泉人罕至其國樂有中國高
麗二部刀楯弓矢以鐵爲鏃挽射矢不能遠詰其故以
其國中不習戰鬭有屋宇父母兄弟臥息異處飲食用
俎豆嫁娶不持錢帛死有棺無槨封土爲冢初喪哭泣
不食肉已葬舉家入水澡浴以祓不祥舉大事則灼骨
諸蕃志卷上
照曠閣

Records of Japanese timber transported to Quanzhou for sale in *A Description of Barbarian Nations, Records of Foreign People* by Zhao Rushi

In the Southern Song Dynasty, Japanese business people often sailed to Quanzhou, Fujian for trade.

The goods transported to Japan by Song Dynasty ships were brocade, silk, spices, porcelain (tea bowls), medicinal materials, books, stationery, copper coins, etc., and the goods transported back from Japan were gold, gulch-gold, beads, mercury, velvet antlers, sulfur, screw heads, timber, handicrafts, swords, folding fans, screens, etc.

During the Song and Yuan Dynasties, Fujian kept close contact with the Goryeo Dynasty on the Korean Peninsula. The goods transported by Song Dynasty ships to the Korean Peninsula were mainly musical instruments, dresses, gold and silver wares, porcelain, lacquerware, Zhejiang silk, Sichuan brocade, aloe, tea, wine, ivory, tortoiseshell, coins, etc. And the goods transported back from the Korean Peninsula mainly included fine horses, weapons, bows and arrows, ginseng, sulfur, medicinal materials, etc.

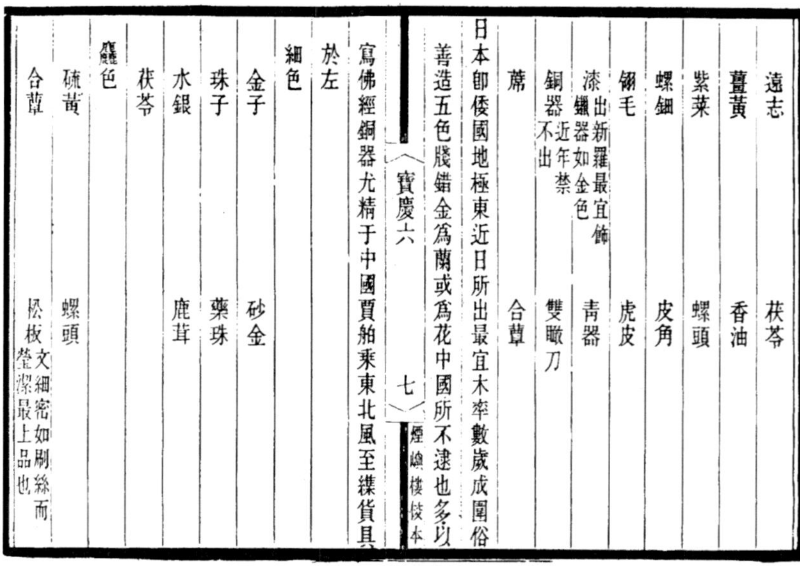
遠志 茯苓
薑黃 香油
紫菜 螺頭
螺鈿 皮角
翎毛 虎皮
漆 出新羅最宜飾鑞器如金色 青器
銅器 近年禁不出 雙瞰刀
蓆 合蕈
日本即倭國地極東近日所出最宜木率數歲成圍俗
善造五色牋銷金為蘭或為花中國所不逮也多以
（寶慶六 七） 煙嶼樓校本
寫佛經銅器尤精于中國賈舶乘東北風至鏶貨具
於左
細色
金子 砂金
珠子 藥珠
水銀 鹿茸
茯苓
麤色
硫黃 螺頭
合蕈 松板 文細密如刷絲而瑩潔最上品也

⦿ The records of the main commodity types imported to Quanzhou from Japan in the *Siming Gazetteer of the Baoqing Period* of the Song Dynasty

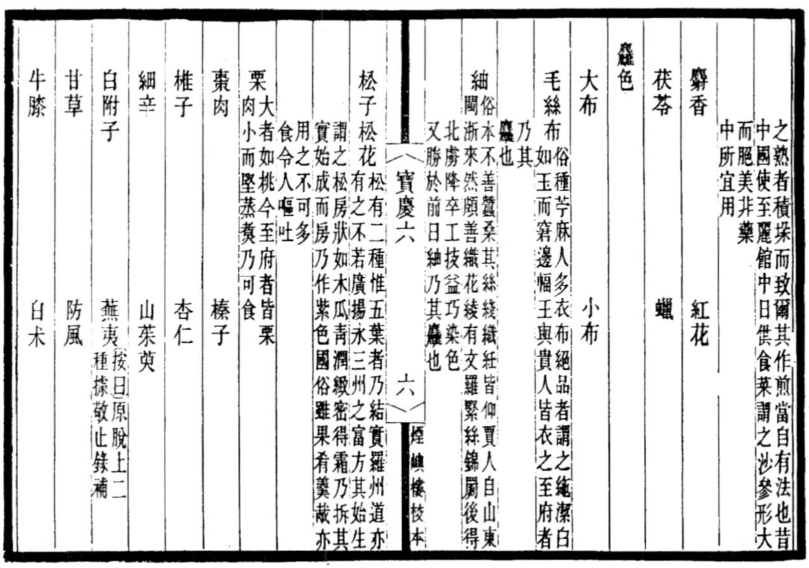
之熟者積垛而致爾其作煎當自有法也昔
中國使至麗館中日供食菜謂之沙參形大
而肥美非藥
中所宜用
麝香 紅花
茯苓 蠟
麤色
大布 小布
毛絲布 俗種苧麻人多衣布絕品者謂之絁潔白
如玉而窄邊幅王與貴人皆衣之至府者
乃其
麤也
紬 俗本不善蠶桑其絲綫織紝皆仰賈人自山東
閩浙來然頗善織花綾有文羅緊絲錦罽後得
北虜降卒工技益巧染色
又勝於前日紬乃其麤也
（寶慶六 六） 煙嶼樓校本
松子 松有二種惟五葉者乃結實羅州道亦
松花 有之不若廣揚永三州之富方其始生
謂之松房狀如木瓜青潤緻密得霜乃拆其
實始成而房乃作紫色國俗雖果肴羹胾亦
用之不可多
食令人嘔吐
栗 大者如桃今至府者皆栗
肉小而堅蒸羹乃可食
棗肉 榛子
椎子 杏仁
細辛 山茱萸
白附子 蕪荑 按日原脫上二
種據敬止錄補
甘草 防風
牛膝 白朮

⦿ Records of Goguryeo's purchase of silk fabrics from Fujian during the Northern Song Dynasty in the *Siming Gazetteer of the Baoqing Period* of the Song Dynasty

At that time, ceramic manufacturing in Fujian was rather developed. There were porcelain kilns everywhere from the coast to the inland. Therefore, the goods exported overseas, in addition to silk, included a large number of ceramic ware. In the 1970s and 1980s, a great many ceramic wares that were salvaged from the sunken ship in the waters of South Korea were products made in Jian kilns, the typical types (tea bowls and cups). The prosperity of the trade between Fujian and Korean Peninsula was undeniable.

As per the records of the *History of Goryeo*, Quanzhou merchants were the most among the merchants engaged in trade in Goryeo in the Song Dynasty. From 1015 to 1090, there were 27 batches of merchant fleets of the Song Dynasty trading on the Korean Peninsula, including 16 from Quanzhou, more than half of the total. As per historical records, the King of Goryeo hosted a banquet for 105 guests, including Quanzhou maritime businessman Huang Zhen during the Cold Food Festival in February 1055.

⦿ Jian zhan (Tea bowl)

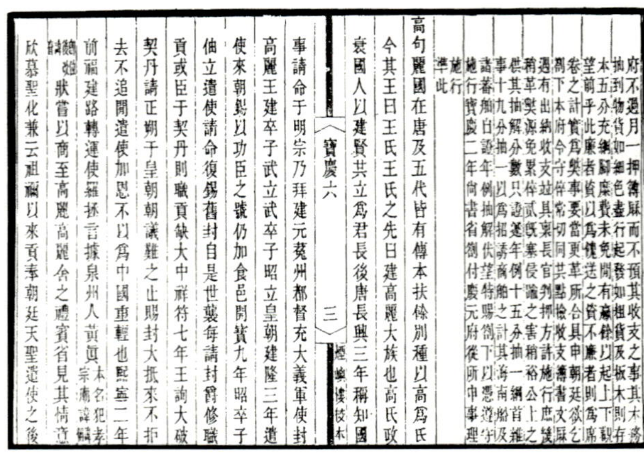

施行準此

高句麗國在唐及五代皆有傳本扶餘别種以高爲氏
今其王曰王氏王氏之先曰建高麗大族也高氏政
衰國人以建賢共立爲君長後唐長興三年稱知國

寶慶六 三

事請命于明宗乃拜建元菟州都督充大義軍使封
高麗王建卒子武立武卒子昭立皇朝建隆三年遣
使來朝賜以功臣之號仍加食邑開寶九年昭卒子
伷立遣使請命復錫舊封自是世襲每請封爵修職
貢或臣于契丹則職貢缺大中祥符七年王詢大破
契丹請正朔于皇朝朝議難之止賜封大抵來不拒
去不追間遣使加恩不以爲中國重輕也熙寧二年
前福建路轉運使羅拯言據泉州人黃眞本名犯孝宗廟諱輒
[illegible]狀嘗以商至高麗高麗舍之禮賓省見其情意
欵慕聖化兼云祖禰以來貢事朝廷天聖遣使之後

⦿ Records of Huang Zhen, a businessman from Quanzhou, going to Goryeo for business in the *Siming Gazetteer of the Baoqing Period* of the Song Dynasty

At that time, many Goryeo business people sailed to Quanzhou for business as well. For example, Guangjin, a native of Luozhou Island in Goryeo, and over ten disciples sailed to Quanzhou for business in 1134.

Song Dynasty China and Goryeo conveyed the intention of cultural exchange through Fujian business people to build a friendship.

The principal goods Fujian exported to Japan and the Korean Peninsula in the Song Dynasty were textile products, porcelain, medicinal materials, spices, books, as well as various daily necessities and cultural supplies. Even Chinese coins were taken to Japan in large quantities. The business contacts between Fujian business people and Japan and Korean Peninsula in the Song Dynasty promoted economic and cultural development and exchange in Northeast Asia.

In the period between the Yuan Dynasty and the Ming Dynasty, Japan was between the end of the Kamakura Shogunate and Northern and Southern Courts. The continuous domestic wars forced many armed groups of warriors and peasants on the west coast of Kyushu to invade China's coastal areas and the Korean Peninsula for survival. They plundered rich and poor alike, which earned them the name Japanese pirates. The social and economic order in China's coastal areas, including Fujian, was seriously disturbed and damaged.

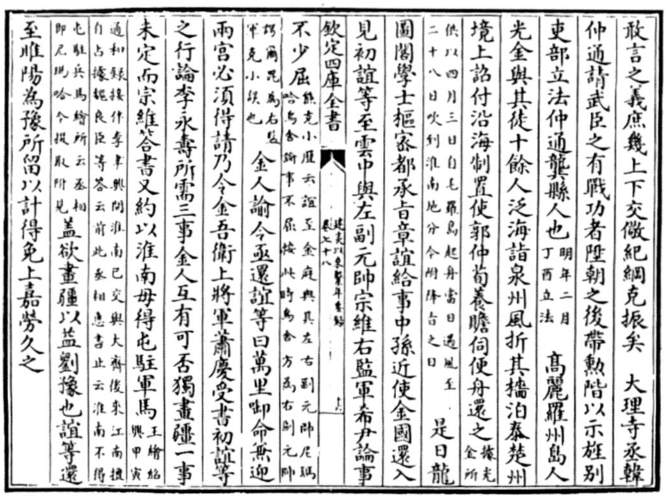

敵言之義庶幾上下交儆紀綱克振矣　大理寺丞韓
仲通請武臣之有戰功者陞朝之後帶勳階以示旌別
吏部立法仲通龔縣人也明年二月丁酉立法　高麗羅州島人
光金與其徒十餘人泛海詣泉州風折其檣泊泰楚州
境上詔付沿海制置使郭仲荀養贍伺便舟還之據光金所
供以四月三日自毛羅島起舟當日遇風至二十八日吹到淮南地分今附降旨之日　是日龍
圖閣學士樞密都承旨章誼給事中孫近使金國還入
見初誼等至雲中與左副元帥宗維右監軍希尹論事
欽定四庫全書　建炎以來繫年要錄　卷七十八
不少屈熊克小曆云誼至金庭與其左右副元帥尼瑪哈烏舍論事不屈按此時烏舍方為右副元帥尼瑪哈為右監軍克小誤也　金人諭令亟還誼等曰萬里啣命無迎
兩宮必須得請乃令金吾衛上將軍蕭慶受書初誼等
之行論李永壽所需三事金人互有可否獨畫疆一事
未定而宗維答書又約以淮南毋得屯駐軍馬王繪紹興甲寅
通和錄載李聿興問淮南已交與大齊後來江南擅自占據恐臣等答云前此未相悉書止云淮南不得
屯駐兵馬繪所云丞相卽尼瑪哈今據取所見　蓋欲畫疆以益劉豫也誼等還
至淮陽為豫所留以計得免上嘉勞久之

⦿ The records of Guangjin, a native of Luozhou Island in Korea, and over ten of his disciples, who traveled to Quanzhou by sea in *Annual Records of the Most Important Events Since the Jianyan Reign-period*

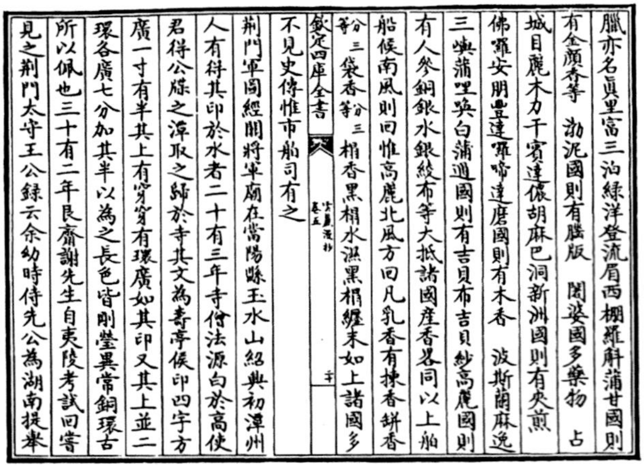

臘亦名貢里富三沟緑洋登流眉西棚羅斛蒲甘國則
有金顔香等　渤泥國則有腦版　闍婆國多藥物　占
城目麗木力千賓達儂胡麻巴洞新洲國則有夾煎
佛羅安朋豊達羅啼達磨國則有木香　波斯蘭麻逸
三嶼蒲哩喚白蒲邇國則有吉貝布吉貝紗高麗國則
有人參銅銀水銀綾布等大抵諸國產香畧同以上舶
船候南風則回惟高麗北風方回凡乳香有揀香缾香
分三等袋香分三等榻香黒榻水濕黒榻纏末如上諸國多
欽定四庫全書　雲麓漫抄
不見史傳惟市舶司有之
荊門軍圖經删将軍廟在當陽縣王水山紹興初漳州
人有得其印於水者二十有三年寺僧法源白於高使
君得公牒之源取之歸於寺其文為壽亭侯印四字方
廣一寸有半其上有穿穿有環廣如其印又其上並二
環各廣七分加其半以為之長色皆剝瑩異常銅環古
所以佩也三十有二年艮齋謝先生自夷陵考試回嘗
見之荊門太守王公録云余幼時侍先公為湖南提舉

⦿ The records of Goryeo merchants bringing ginseng to Quanzhou in *Yunlu Manchao*

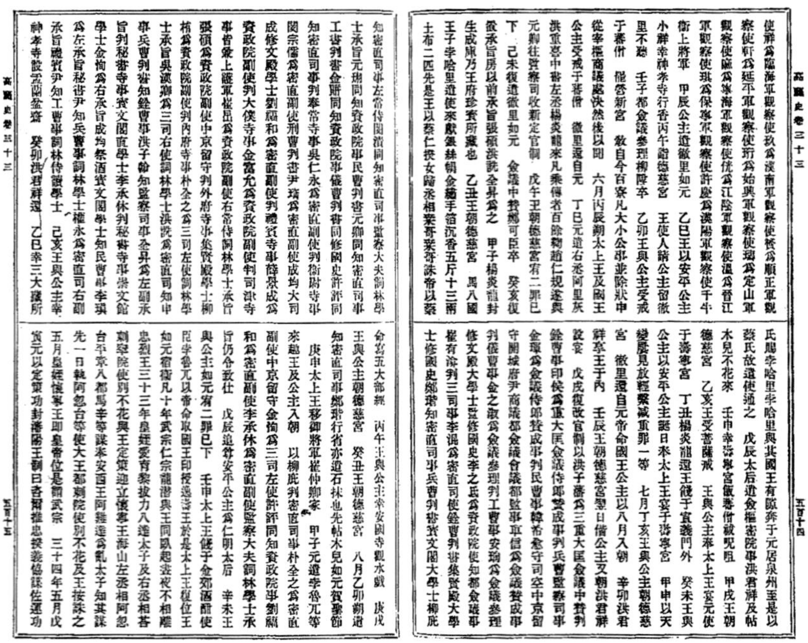

⦿ The records of the Prince of the Chola Dynasty in India settled in Quanzhou and did business with Goryeo in the *History of Goryeo*

⦿ Fine brocade of Song Dynasty exported to Japan and Goryeo

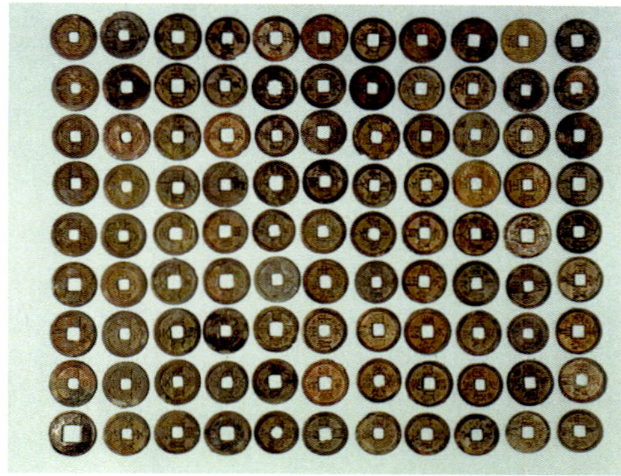

⦿ A large amount of Song Dynasty currency exported to Japan

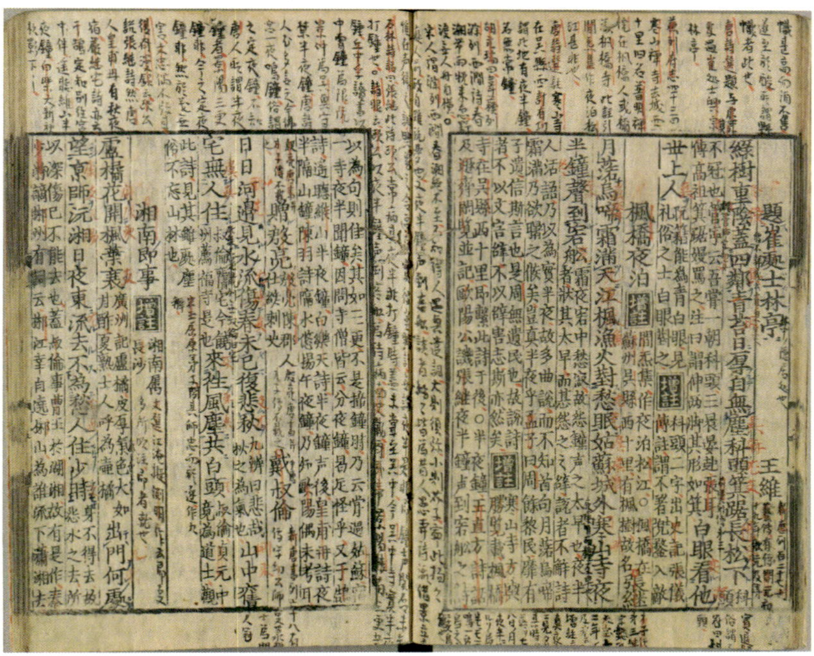

題崔處士林亭 王維
綠樹重陰蓋四鄰青苔日厚自無塵科頭箕踞長松下白眼看他世上人

楓橋夜泊
月落烏啼霜滿天江楓漁火對愁眠姑蘇城外寒山寺夜半鐘聲到客船

贈殷亮 戴叔倫
日日河邊見水流傷春未已復悲秋山中舊宅無人住來往風塵共白頭

湘南即事
盧橘花開楓葉衰出門何處望京師沅湘日夜東流去不為愁人住少時

⦿ Books of the Song Dynasty bought by Japan, sample pages

2 Thriving Trade

During the Ming and Qing Dynasties, the central court implemented a ban on maritime trade or intercourse with foreign countries, but it never curbed the development of Fujian's maritime trade economy. Fujian merchants had grown from the official tributary trade in the early Ming Dynasty to the free merchants in the middle Ming Dynasty, and to the maritime groups by the end of the Ming Dynasty. Their efforts pushed the Fujian Maritime Silk Road to its peak. Their footprints extended beyond Fujian and Taiwan, reaching Japan in the east, Myanmar in the west, the Liaodong Peninsula in the north, and the Lesser Sunda Islands in the south. A wide business network was established in this area, and they became the backbone force of China's Maritime Silk Road in the Ming and Qing Dynasties. And Japan, which is close to Fujian, became one of the important bases for Fujian business people to gather and do business.

⦿ *Illustrated Handbook of Japanese Pirates*, collected by the Compilation Institute of Historical Materials, University of Tokyo, Japan

⦿ Picture of Japanese pirates and their ships harassing China's coastal areas and the Korean Peninsula

⦿ Picture of the Navy of Zhejiang and Fujian defending against Japanese pirates

⦿ The portrait of Sakugen Shūryō, a famous monk and envoy sent by Japan

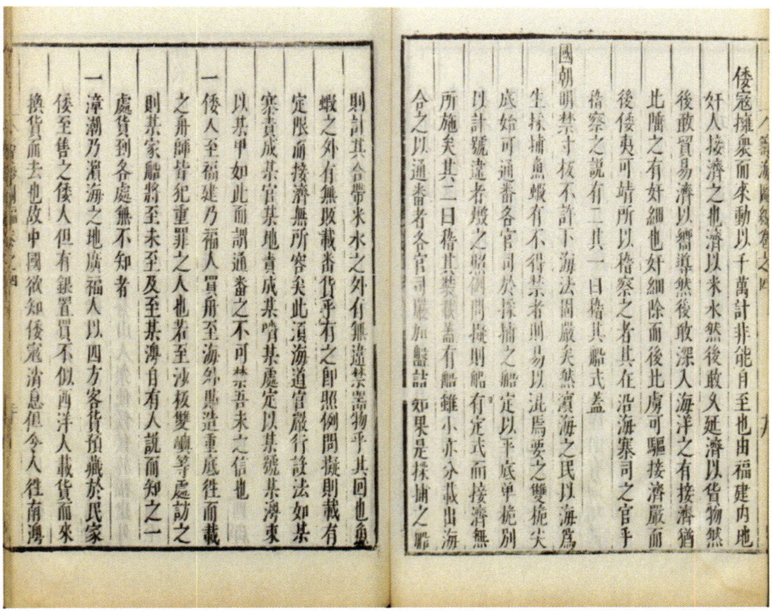

倭寇擁衆而來動以千萬計非能自至也由福建內地
奸人接濟之也濟以米水然後敢久延濟以貨物然
後敢貿易濟以嚮導然後敢深入海洋之有接濟猶
北陲之有奸細也奸細除而後北虜可驅接濟嚴而
後倭夷可靖所以稽察之者其在沿海寨司之官乎
稽察之說有二其一曰稽其船式蓋
國朝明禁寸板不許下海法固嚴矣然濱海之民以海爲
生採捕魚蝦有不得禁者則易以混焉要之雙桅尖
底始可通番各官司於採捕之船定以平底單桅別
以計號違者照例問擬則船有定式而接濟無
所施矣其二曰稽其裝載蓋有船雖小亦分載出海
合之以通番者各官司嚴加盤詰如果是採捕之船
則計其合帶米水之外有無違禁器物乎其回也魚
蝦之外有無販載番貨乎有之即照例問擬則載有
定限而接濟無所容矣此須海道官嚴行設法如某
寨責成某官某地責成某哨某處定以某號某澳束
以某甲如此而謂通番之不可禁吾未之信也
一倭人至福建乃福人買舟至海外與造重底徃而載
之舟師皆犯重罪之人也若至沙板雙桅等處訪之
則某家船將至未至及至某澳自有人說而知之一
處貨到各處無不知者
一漳潮乃濱海之地廣福人以四方客貨預藏於民家
倭至售之倭人但有銀置買不似西洋人載貨而來
換貨而去也故中國欲知倭寇消息但令人往南澳

⦿ The records of the people of Zhangquan in Fujian Province in the early Ming Dynasty colluding with Japanese pirates in *Chou Hai Tu Bian*

During the Yongle years (1403–1422) of the Ming Dynasty, the Chinese imperial court once established a suzerain-vassal relationship with the samurai regime controlled by the shogunate of Muromachi in Japan. Both parties maintained China-centered trade for over 100 years. To a certain extent, this type of trade restrained the invasion of Japanese pirates. In 1407, the Yongle Emperor conferred the title of nobility on Ashikaga Yoshimitsu, the shogun of Muromachi, as the Japanese king.

The export of copper coins, raw silk, cotton silk, silk, ceramics, spices, and Buddhist books to Japan and the import of copper, sulfur, gold, swords, lacquerware, and clay paintings from Japan characterized the Sino-Japanese trade of this period.

⦿ Restoration model of Japan's early ships sent to Ming China

⦿ Picture of ships Japan sent to Ming China in the later period, collected by Shinshōgokuraku-ji

During the Chenghua years (1465–1487) of the Ming Dynasty, Xin Fang, the deputy inspector, was ordered to inspect the seaway and discovered that Fujian's private maritime smuggling was rather developed. During this period, the smuggling took place mostly in Zhangquan coastal area, the import and export markets and Southeast Asian countries, and Ryukyu.

Emperor of the Ming Dynasty Record, *Huangming Xiangxu Records* by Mao Ruizheng and *Chongxiang Collection* by Dong Yingju all documented the historical fact that a large number of Zhangquan merchants travelled to Japan for trade, drifted to the Korean Peninsula, and were escorted back to China in the middle of Ming Dynasty.

⦿ Seal, the authorized official seal of the shogunate administration in the silk trade among Japanese, Fujian, and Zhejiang ships

⦿ The seal of the Japanese king given by the Ming Dynasty court to Ashikaga Yoshimitsu, and the portrait of Ashikaga Yoshimitsu in the Mōri Museum of Yamaguchi, Japan

⦿ Special prints

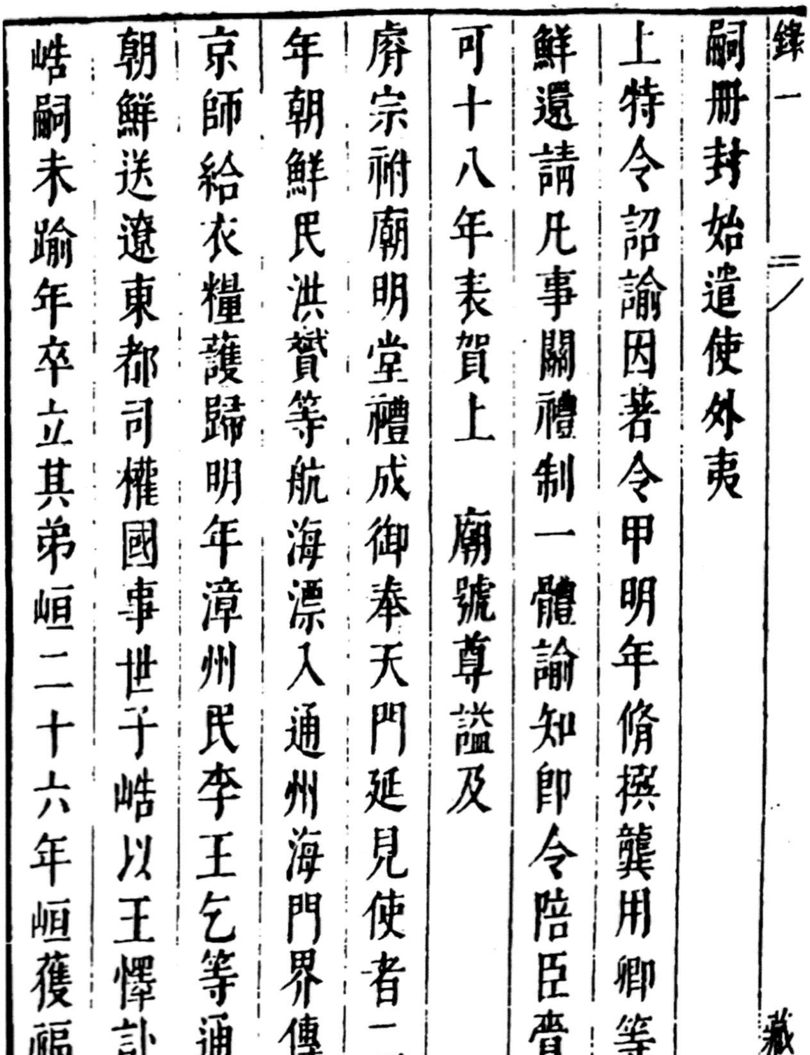
錄一　二　藏板

嗣冊封始遣使外夷
上特令詔諭因著令甲明年脩撰龔用卿等使朝
鮮還請凡事關禮制一體諭知即令陪臣賫示報
可十八年表賀上　廟號尊謚及
睿宗祔廟明堂禮成御奉天門延見使者二十三
年朝鮮民洪贇等航海漂入通州海門界傳詣
京師給衣糧護歸明年漳州民李王乞等通番漂
朝鮮送遼東都司權國事世子峼以王懌訃來告
峼嗣未踰年卒立其弟峘二十六年峘獲福清通

⊙ The record of Zhangquan merchants who travelled to Japan for trade, drifted to the Korean Peninsula and were escorted back to China in 1547 in *Huangming Xiangxu Records of the Emperor of the Ming Dynasty*

Having seen the development of the commodity economy in southeast coastal areas and the rising demand for sea trade of people in Fujian and Guangdong coastal areas, the Imperial Court eventually approved the petition of Fujian governor Tu Zemin to lift the ban on maritime trade or intercourse with foreign countries in the first year of the Longqing Period of the Ming Dynasty (1567).

With the ban lifted, private maritime trade in Fujian coastal areas rose again and thrived, and the maritime exchanges between Fujian and Northeast Asian countries happened with increased frequency. During this period, Chinese ships, Ryukyu ships, Nanban ships, and Luzon ships maintained frequent business ties with the ports of Bōnotsu and Yamagawa in the south of Kyushu.

⦿ The maritime merchant Wang Hou's old residence in Xiangyu village of the Changle County in the Ming Dynasty

⦿ The ferry site of Xiangyu village, Changle District, Fuzhou City, where there were business people who sailed to Japan for trade in the middle of Ming Dynasty

In 1596, Fujiwara Seika (teacher of Tokugawa Ieyasu and Hayashi Razan), who was known as the first person of Cheng-zhu school in Modern Japan, recorded in his diary, *Fragmentary Notes of The Voyages Southwards*, the busy and multifaceted trade of Fuji merchants among China's coastal areas, Southeast Asia and Japan.

After the middle of Ming Dynasty, the western colonists reached the East and invaded the major ports of South and Southeast Asia. The trading ships of Fujian maritime merchants had to change their business area from the Indian Ocean to the east of Malacca Strait. At this point, the Japanese social economy welcomed great development.

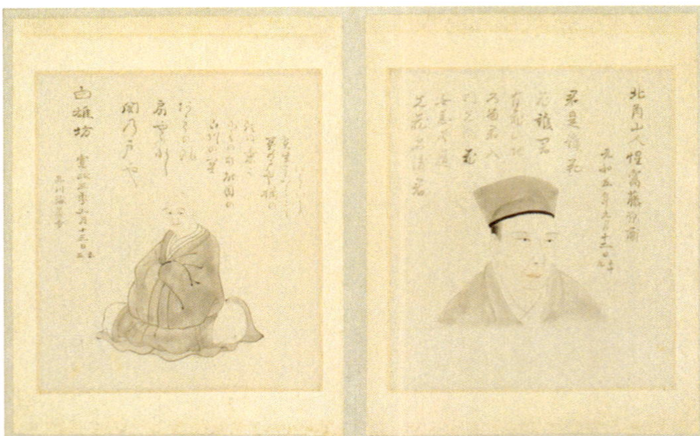

⦿ *Fragmentary Notes of The Voyages Southwards*, sample pages

⦿ Portrait of Fujiwara Seika, collected by Tokyo National Museum, Japan

⦿ Inscription on the plaque on the inside of the first peak gate of Sōfuku-ji temple in Nagasaki, Japan, by Lin Taiqing

Gold and silver mines were exploited in large quantities. The nobles and samurai were proud of owning Chinese goods. The huge demand in Japanese market for Chinese handicrafts attracted a large number of Fujian merchants to sell goods to Japan. The trade of Fujian merchants was characterized by the expansion of market and trading activities in Luzon, Japan and China's coastal areas during this period.

In 1609, Lin Taiqing, the owner of Fuqing maritime vessels, crossed the sea to Kagoshima, married a local and started a family. In 1619, his family moved to Nagasaki. The plaque on the inside of the first peak gate of Sōfuku-ji Temple in Nagasaki was inscribed by Lin. The plaque is a provincial cultural relic of Nagasaki.

Lin Shoudian (Japanese Name: Hayashi Jinbee), the son of Lin Taiqing, was one of the important figures active in Nagasaki's Sino-Japan trade.

In 1628, He Gaocai, another Fuqing maritime merchant, moved to Nagasaki. He married a Japanese woman and had two sons.

His eldest son, He Zhaojin, took up the post of an interpreter in 1658. He and his son accumulated a lot of wealth by managing Sino-Japan trade. They made a considerable donation to plenty of temples in Nagasaki, the most famous of which is the donation to build the Kiyomizu-dera in Nagasaki.

⦿ During the Wanli years (1573–1620) of the Ming Dynasty, Mōri, the Japanese vassal Lord, issued a flag code to maritime merchants who were surnamed Cai in Jinjiang, Fujian as approval of their trading activities

⦿ Shimizu Temple, Nagasaki, Japan

⦿ Interior of the main hall of Shimizu Temple

⦿ The inscribed plaque of the main hall Shimizu Temple, by Mu'an, an important national cultural relic in Japan

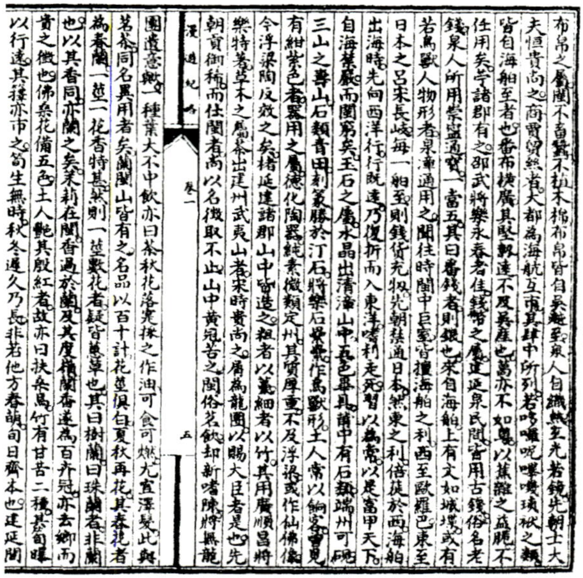
四

布帛之屬閩不畜蠶不植木棉布帛皆自吳越至泉人自織絲玄光若鏡先朝士大
夫恒貴尚之商賈貿絲者大都為海航互市其肆中所列若哆囉呢嗶嘰瑣袱之類
皆自海舶至者也番布橫廣具堅韌遠不及吳產也葛亦不如粵以蕉雞之疏脆不
任用矣宁諸郡有之卲武將樂永春者佳錢幣之屬建延泉民間皆用古錢俗名老
錢泉人所用崇禎通寶一當五其曰番錢者則銀也來自海舶上有文如城堞或有
若鳥獸人物形者泉漳通用之閩往時閩中巨室皆擅海舶之利西至歐羅巴東至
日本之呂宋長崎每一舶至則錢貨充牣先朝禁通日本然東之利倍蓰於西海舶
出海時先向西洋行行既遠乃復折而入東洋嗜利走死習以為常以是富甲天下
自海禁嚴而閩窮矣玉石之屬水晶出清漳山中五色畢具其中有石類端州可硯
三山之壽山石類青田刻篆勝於汀石將樂石琢作鳥獸形土人常以餉客曾見
有紺紫色者器用之屬德化陶器純素緻類定州其質厚重不及浮梁或作仙佛像
令浮梁陶反效之矣楮延建諸郡山中皆造之粗者以蓑細者以竹其用廣順昌將
樂特著草木之屬茶出建州武夷山者宋時貴尚之爲爲龍團以賜大臣者是也先
朝貢御稀而仕閩者尚以名徵取不止山中黃冠苦之閩俗茗飲却新嗜陳將興龍

漫遊紀略 卷一 五

團遺意歟一種葉大不中飲亦曰茶秋花落兒揉之作油可食可燃尤宜澤髮此與
茗茶同名異用者矣蘭閩山皆有之名品以百十計花莖俱白夏秋再花其春花者
為春蘭一莖一花香特甚然則一莖數花者疑皆蕙草也其曰樹蘭曰珠蘭者非蘭
也以其香同亦蘭之矣茉莉在閩香過於蘭及其度嶺蘭香遂為百卉冠亦去鄉而
貴之徵也佛桑花備五色土人艷其殷紅者故亦曰扶桑島竹有甘苦二種其筍曜
以行遠其篠亦市之筍生無時秋冬逾久乃長非若他方春萌旬日齋本也建延閩

⦿ The records of private merchants trading in Fujian, Japan, and Luzon in Wang Shengshi's *Sailing History* in the Qing Dynasty

⦿ Lantern stone, originally used as the stone pillar of the wharf, Buddhist clock of Shimizu Temple in Nagasaki, Japan, funded by the donations of Fujian business people He Gaocai and Wei Zhiyan

The Chinese literature has widely recorded the increasing number of Fujian people who stayed and emigrated to Japan for business.

At the turn from the Ming Dynasty to the Qing Dynasty, many Fujianese who migrated to Nagasaki, Japan, died in that foreign country. Local relatives or overseas Chinese buried them near Kōshin-ji Temple in Nazuo Mountain, west of Nagasaki port. Most of them were from Fuqing, Changle, Fuzhou, and southern Fujian.

⦿ Tombs of the deceased Chinese

⦿ The cemetery in Inazo international cemetery, Nagasaki, Japan, for those who were born in Fuzhou

⦿ The tombstone in Inazo international tombstone, Nagasaki, Japan listing the dead who were born in Tong'an

⦿ Tombstones of those who were born in Fuqing

⦿ Tombstone of the dead, who were born in Fujian

3 The Fujian Officials in Goryeo

In ancient times, Fujian merchant ships reached northward to Jiangsu, Zhejiang, Shandong, Liaodong, the Korean Peninsula, and the Japanese archipelago, and southward to Southeast Asian countries through the South China Sea. The Fujianese made full use of this geographical advantage to build a friendship with the Korean Peninsula. In the Song Dynasty, they played an important role in the interaction between China and Goryeo.

During the Xining period (1068–1077) of the Song Dynasty, Goryeo attempted to pay tribute to the Northern Song Dynasty. It applied for entry via the Quanzhou road in Fujian Province. The court approved the visit only if they entered the country through Mingzhou (now Ningbo City in Zhejiang Province) and Runzhou (now Zhenjiang City in Jiangsu Province).

Upon the establishment of the suzerain-vassal relationship, the two countries maintained close relations and frequent official and civilian exchanges. Goryeo sent students to China many times to study Chinese culture.

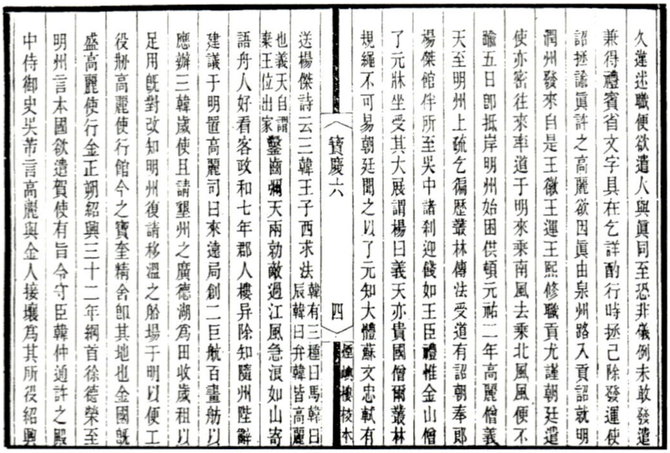
久違述職便欲遣人與眞同至恐非儀例未敢發遣
兼得禮賓省文字具在乞詳酌行時拯已除發運使
詔拯諭眞許之高麗欲因眞由泉州路入貢詔就明
潤州發來自是王徽王運王熙修職貢尤謹朝廷遣
使亦密往來率道于明來乘南風去乘北風風便不
踰五日即抵岸明州始困供頓元祐二年高麗僧義
天至明州上疏乞徧歷叢林傳法受道有詔朝奉郎
楊傑館伴所至吳中諸刹迎餞如王臣禮惟金山僧
了元牀坐受其大展謂楊曰義天亦貴國僧爾叢林
規繩不可易朝廷聞之以了元知大體蘇文忠軾有
寶慶六　四　煙嶼樓校本
送楊傑詩云三韓王子西求法（韓有三種曰馬韓曰辰韓曰弁韓皆高麗）
也義天自謂棄王位出家）鑿齒彌天兩勍敵過江風急浪如山寄
語舟人好看客政和七年郡人樓异除知隨州陛辭
建議于明置高麗司曰來遠局創二巨航百畫舫以
應辦三韓歲使且請墾州之廣德湖爲田收歲租以
足用既對改知明州復請移溫之船場于明以便工
役掛高麗使行館今之寶奎精舍即其地也金國既
盛高麗使行金正朔紹興三十二年綱首徐德榮至
明州言本國欲遣賀使有旨令守臣韓仲通許之殿
中侍御史吳芾言高麗與金人接壤爲其所役紹興

⦿ Records of Goryeo applying to enter China from Quanzhou in Fujian Province in the *Siming Gazetteer of the Baoqing Period* of the Song Dynasty

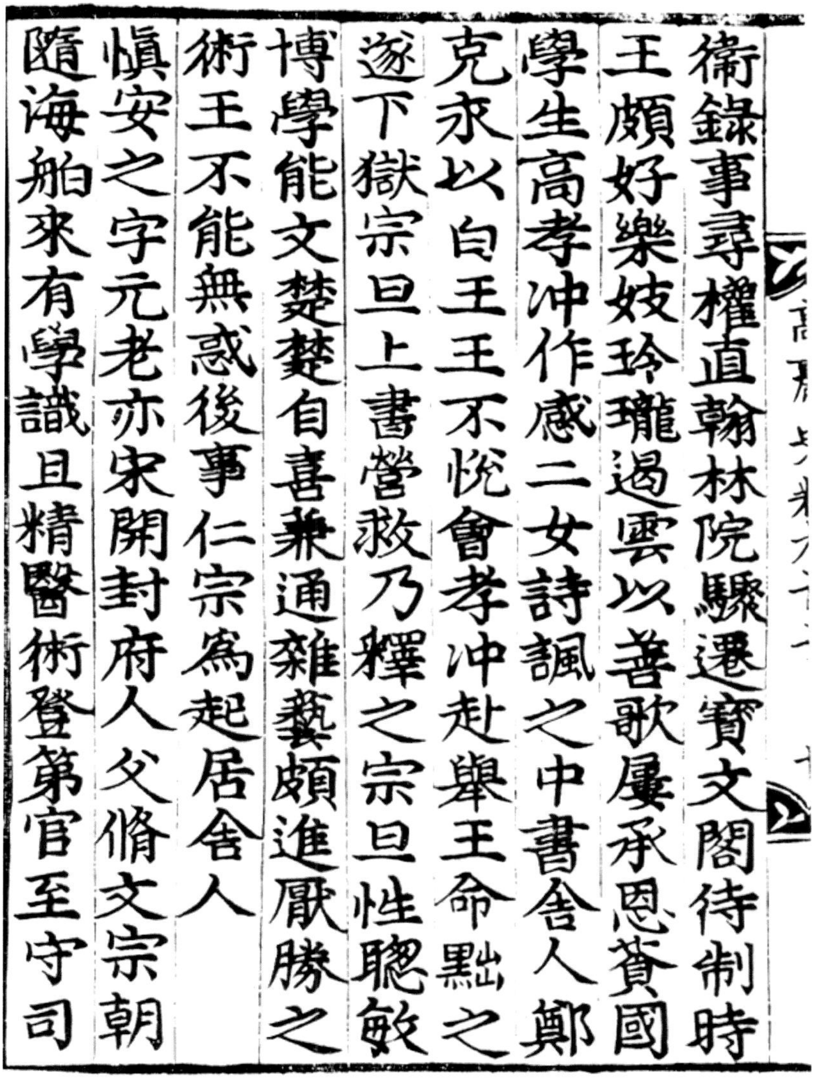
衛錄事尋權直翰林院驟遷寶文閣待制時
王頗好樂妓玲瓏遏雲以善歌屢承恩賚國
學生高孝冲作感二女詩諷之中書舍人鄭
克求以白王王不悅會孝冲赴舉王命黜之
遂下獄宗旦上書營救乃釋之宗旦性聰敏
博學能文楚楚自喜兼通雜藝頗進厭勝之
術王不能無惑後事仁宗爲起居舍人
愼安之字元老亦宋開封府人父脩文宗朝
隨海舶來有學識且精醫術登第官至守司

◉ The records of Hu Zongdan, a Fuzhou native, who took a position as an official in Goryeo in *History of Goryeo*

4 The Zheng Family and Japan

At the turn from the Ming Dynasty to the Qing Dynasty, there was an active political force on the southeast coast of China, namely the Zheng group under the leadership of Zheng Chenggong. From Zheng Zhilong's active exploration of private maritime trade to Zheng Chenggong's recovery of Taiwan, the group had been closely connected with Japan.

Zheng Zhilong (1604–1661), the founder of the Zheng group, was born in Shijing Town, Nan'an City, Fujian Province. When he was young, he followed his uncle Huang Cheng to Xiangshan'ao, Guangdong Province (today's Macao) to engage in maritime trade. In 1621, he sailed, with the merchant Li Dan, to Japan to trade.

Zheng Chenggong, the son of Zheng Zhilong, took Anping (now Anhai Town, Jinjiang City, Fujian Province) as a stronghold and fought against the Qing Dynasty. He inherited the family business and occupied several cities. As a Chinese Ming loyalist, he resisted the Qing conquest of China and regarded the revival of the Ming Dynasty as his duty.

⦿ The exhibition room of Zheng Zhilong's achievements at the Zheng Chenggong Memorial in Hirado, Japan

⦿ Portrait of Zheng Zhilong

⦿ Hirado, Hizen Province, Japan, the birthplace of Zheng Chenggong.

⦿ Red seal ships of the Araki family. In the early days of Edo, the Araki family traded with Fujian business people in Siam, Annan, and Jiaozhi.

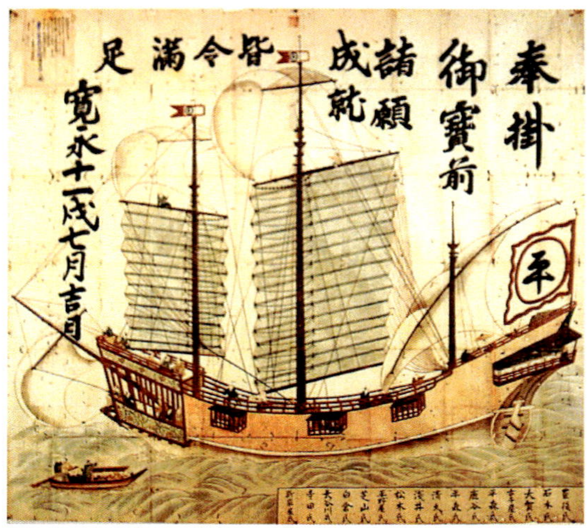

⦿ Red seal ships of the Suetsuku family. In 1624–1643, the Suetsuku family traded with Li Dan in Taiwan and with Fujian business people in Luzon and Annan.

⦿ The statue of Zheng Chenggong and his mother, made by the citizens of Hirado and stored in the memorial hall of Zheng Chenggong, Hirado, Japan

Zheng Chenggong continued large-scale overseas trade so as to finance the army with business interests. Based in Xiamen and Taiwan, Zheng's trade fleet transported Chinese goods to Southeast Asia and Southeast Asian goods to Japan in exchange for military supplies and other goods. Business with Japan has always been the principal trade activity of the Zheng group.

⦿ The portrait of Zheng Chenggong, collected by Zheng Chenggong Memorial, Hirado, Japan

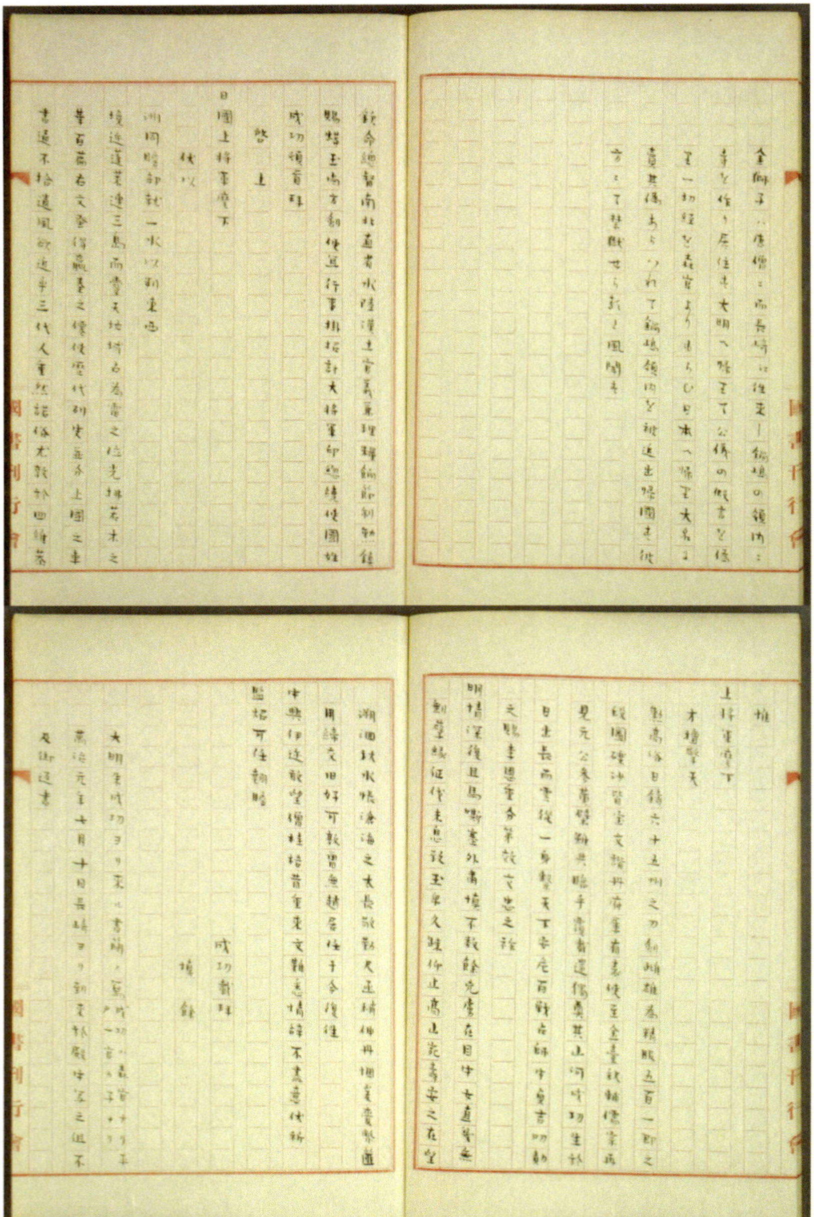

⊙ Zheng Chenggong's letter to a shogun of Bakufu, Japan (transcript), kept in the library of Waseda University, Japan. The date when the transcript was made remains unknown

According to a report by the viceroy of the Dutch East India Company, 57 Chinese ships arrived in Nagasaki, Japan, including 41 Anhai ships (most of which belonged to Zheng Chenggong) from November 1654 to September 1655. The bulk of the cargo on these merchant ships were raw silk, textiles, deerskin, and sugar.

Zheng group dominated the overseas trade of the southeast coast for over 60 years, which greatly promoted the development of overseas Fujian merchants. It was under the influence of Zheng's trade that a large number of Chinatowns appeared in Nagasaki, Manila, and Batavia (now Jakarta, Indonesia).

⦿ Zheng group's bulk commodity exported to Japan was deerskin, raw silk and tough silk

The stories of Zheng Chenggong were noticed by Kabuki playwrights in Japan. In the early 18th century, Japanese dramatist Chikamatsu Monzaemon created the Kabuki drama *The Battles of Coxinga* with Zheng Chenggong as the inspiration. Although most of the plots were badly inconsistent with historical facts, the show was well recognized and adored by the Japanese audience. As a great success, the performance is available and popular today, still.

⦿ *The Battles of Coxinga* lantern for a parade in a festival at Kajichō, Hachinohe, Aomori Prefecture, Japan

⦿ Poster of *The Battles of Coxinga*

5 Legend of Chinese Business People in Nagasaki

Nagasaki, Japan, has been a significant node of the Sino-Northeast-Asian network since the 16th century. It has played an irreplaceable role in the history of Chinese business activities in East Asian waters, the history of Fujian business people emigrating overseas, and the history of Sino-Japanese cultural exchanges.

The trade activities of Fujian business people between Fujian and Nagasaki have a long and continuous history. In the Mid- and Late-Qing Dynasty, as the modern capitalist world economic system expanded globally, Japan opened itself for business. Nagasaki became a major port for foreign trade. Among the groups engaged in commercial activities, the strength of Chinese business people from Jinmen, Fujian Province, was impressive. Among them, Taichang Business was an outstanding representative.

Taichang Business was founded in 1862. It had earned a fine reputation in Nagasaki. The shareholders from Tong'an, Fujian Province (now in the area of Tong'an District and Xiang'an District of Xiamen City, Fujian Province) and Kinmen co-financed it. It was mainly engaged in goods transportation and marketing, packaging for customers, and an exchange agency. In the heyday of the Taichang Business, it attracted customers from virtually all of East Asia, from Vladivostok, Russia, to Singapore.

When the Nagasaki port opened, the Fujianese set up the Fujian Guild in the China Guild in order to ensure their own interests. Fundamentally, it aimed to unite the bond strength of local businesses and standardize business operations. In other words, it is through the credibility of organizations like the Fujian Guild, in combination with the advantages of geography, industry, and luck, that the Fujian business groups were able to connect Northeast Asia, East China, and Southeast Asia into a giant business circle, to take root in the East Asian business, and to make brilliant achievements.

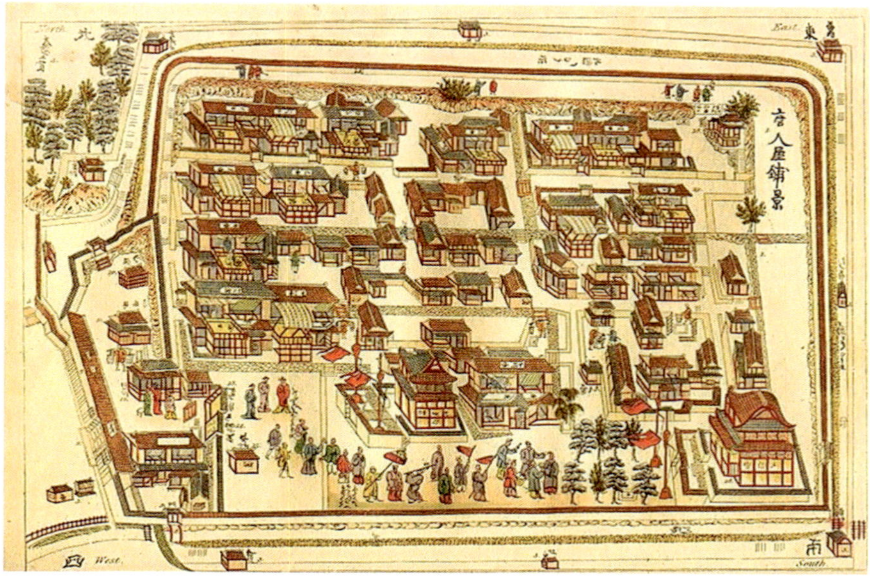

⦿ The Chinese Hall where Chinese merchants gathered in Nagasaki, Japan, 1689–1858

⦿ Taichang account book

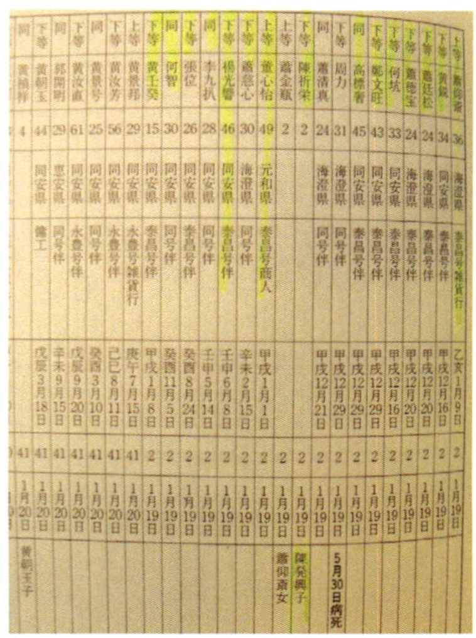

⦿ A list of Fujian merchants who immigrated to Nagasaki, Japan from 1868 to 1875

⦿ Fujian Guild hall in Nagasaki, Japan

⦿ Thien Hau Temple in Nagasaki, Japan (built in 1736)

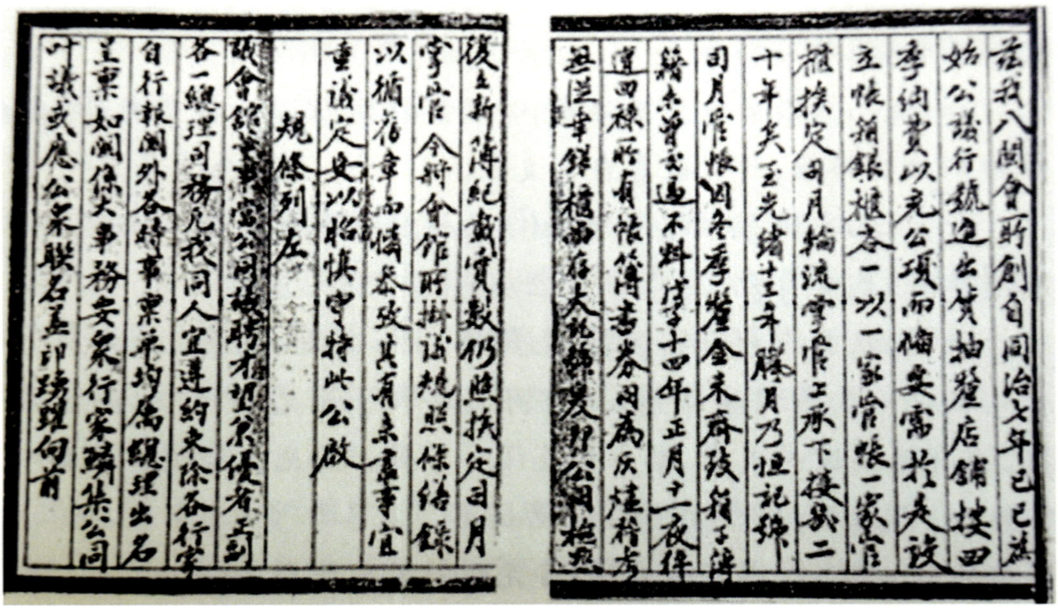

茲我八閩會所創自同治七年己巳孟
始公議行號進出貨抽釐店鋪按四
季納費以充公項而備要需於是設
立帳簿錄總各一以一家管帳一家管
總按定司月輪流掌管互承下接計二
十年矣至光緒十三年臘月乃將記錄
司月掌帳因各季釐金未齊致簿子未
繳去曾武通不料光緒十四年正月十一夜伴
遭回祿一所有帳簿簿書券因為灰燼稽考
無從幸錄總簿存大龍號[illegible]公同[illegible]

後立新簿紀載實數仍照按定司月
掌管今將會館所擬議規照條錄錄
以循存章而備參考其有未盡事宜
重議定是以昭慎重特此公啟

規條列左

一 福建會館[illegible]公司[illegible]聘有經理[illegible]者[illegible]
各一總理司務凡我同人宜遵約束除各行家
自行報關外各時事案並均爲總理出名
呈稟如關係大事務要衆行家齊集公同
計議或應公衆聯名蓋印務須向首

⦿ *Regulations of the Fujian Guild*, sample pages

Fujianese Association heeds to both the establishment of commercial norms and the inheritance of traditional Chinese local spirit, religious beliefs, and rituals.

⦿ Picture of Welcome the Statue of Mazu

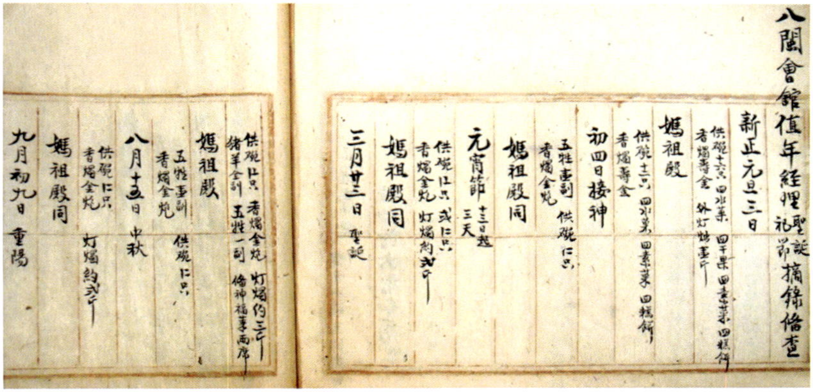

⦿ The ritual book of the Fujian Guild in Nagasaki, Japan

⊙ God of Land Temple (built in 1691)

⊙ Guan Yu Hall (built in 1736)

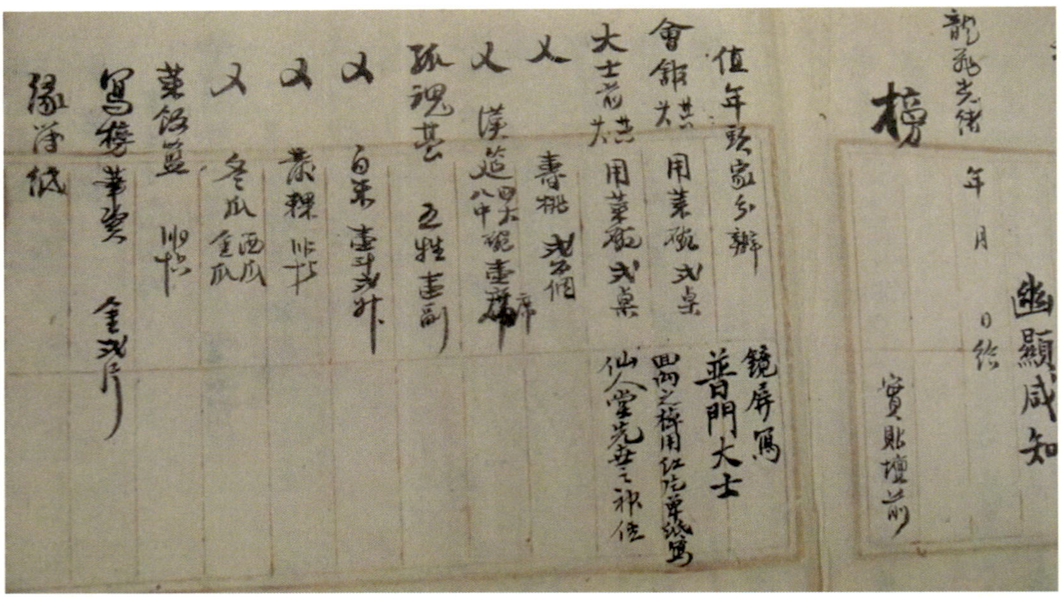

榜

幽顯咸知

鏡屛寫

普門大士

⊙ Supply list of the Zhongyuan Festival for the rituals at the Fujian Guild

CHAPTER 4

SHIPS, PORTS, AND SEA ROUTES

The Maritime Silk Road between Fujian and Northeast Asia is composed of ships, harbors and sea routes. Ships engaged in trade in this region came from China, Japan, Korea, Ryukyu, and even Europe. The prosperity of maritime trade in Northeast Asia came with famous trade harbors and the fixed trade routes have left clear footprints in history.

1 The Busy Ships

The ships that set sail from Fujian to Northeast Asia are called Tang ships in the literature. In fact, they are divided into Fuzhou ships, Xiamen ships, and Taiwan ships. Also, Ryukyu ships, Nanjing ships, and Ningbo ships were active in trade in this area.

1.1 Fuzhou ships, Xiamen ships, and Taiwan ships

Per ancient shipbuilding technology, the wooden sailing ships with similar structure and shape, which were distributed from the south of Zhejiang Province in the north to the east of Guangdong Province in the south, were generally labeled Fu ships. With stable performance against strong winds and waves, they were deemed the best long-distance ship in southeast coastal areas of China. And the representatives of Fu ships were Fuzhou ships, Xiamen ships, and Taiwan ships. The literature of Edo period (1603–1867) in Japan documented and depicted a great number of Chinese ships, especially Fu ships.

⦿ A Fujian merchant ship sailing to Japan for trade

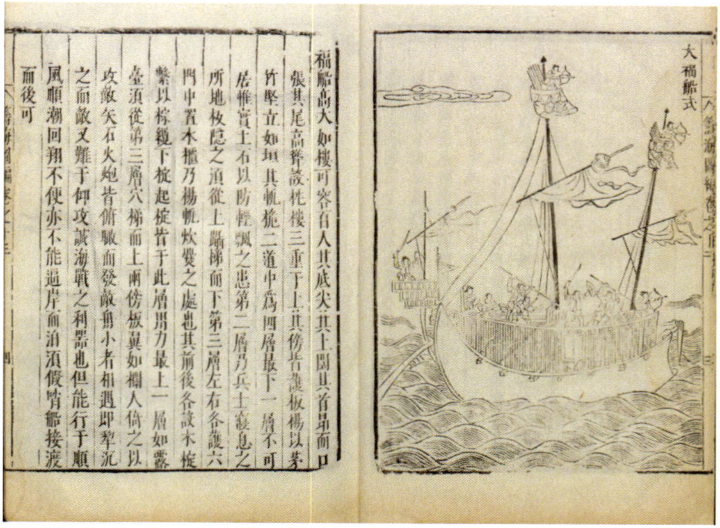

福船高大如樓可容百人其底尖其上闊其首昂而口張其尾高聳設柁樓三重于上其傍皆護板楊以茅竹堅立如垣其帆桅二道中為四層最下一層不可居惟實土石以防輕飄之患第二層乃兵士寢息之所地板隱之須從上躡梯而下第三層左右各護六門中置水櫃乃揚帆炊爨之處也其前後各設木椗繫以棕纜下椗起椗皆于此層用力最上一層如露臺須從第三層穴梯而上兩傍板翼如欄人倚之以攻敵矢石火炮皆俯瞰而發敵舟小者相遇即犁沉之而敵又難于仰攻誠海戰之利器也但能行于順風順潮回翔不便亦不能逼岸而泊須假哨船接渡而後可

The illustration of a big Fu Ship that Qi Jiguang commanded to fight against Japanese pirates recorded in the *Chou Hai Tu Bian*

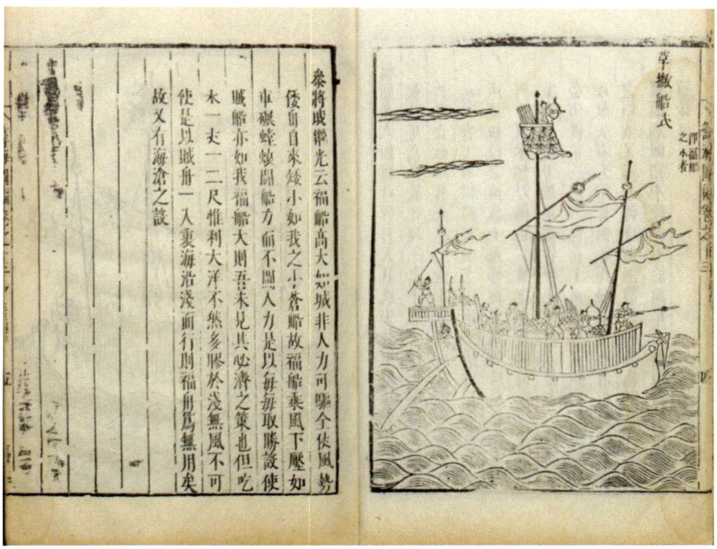

參將戚繼光云福船高大如城非人力可驅全仗風勢倭舟自來矮小如我之小蒼船故福船乘風下壓如車碾螳螂鬪船力而不鬪人力是以每每取勝設使賊船亦如我福船大則吾未見其必濟之策也但吃水一丈一二尺惟利大洋不然多膠於淺無風不可使是以賊舟一入裏海沿淺而行則福舟為無用矣故又有海滄之設

The illustration of a small Fu Ship that Qi Jiguang commanded to fight against Japanese pirates recorded in the *Chou Hai Tu Bian*

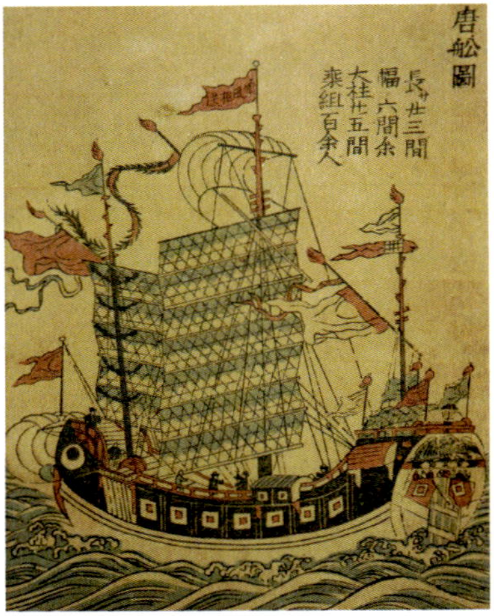

⦿ Tang ship (Fujian ship) in Japanese literature

⦿ Xiamen ship in trade in Nagasaki

⦿ Fuzhou ship arrived in Nagasaki and Japanese unloaded cargo

Xiamen ships were ships entering and leaving from Moon Port of Zhangzhou, except their principal harbor is Xiamen, thus they were mainly engaged in the foreign trade of Xiamen. They shared similarity in structure with Fuzhou ships. The color of the hull is the indicator of the origin of the ships.

Fuzhou ships are oft painted red, while Xiamen ships and Quanzhou ships are usually white. The carrying capacity of Xiamen ships was up to 150 tons.

Taiwan was under the jurisdiction of Fujian in the early days. It was not until 1885 that the province was established. Therefore, most of Taiwan's ships came from Fujian, Fuzhou, or Xiamen. Zheng Chenggong's trading ships were Taiwan ships.

⦿ Taiwan ships sailing to trade in Nagasaki

1.2 Nanjing Ships and Ningbo Ships

Fujian's superb shipbuilding technology and rich shipbuilding resources attracted maritime merchants from all over the world to Fuzhou to entrust shipbuilding to Fujianese shipbuilders, including merchants from Nanjing, Ningbo, Guangdong, Siam, and Ryukyu. Their sails with these giant ships across Southeast Asia, East Asia, and Northeast Asia formed a distinctive Chinese business circle.

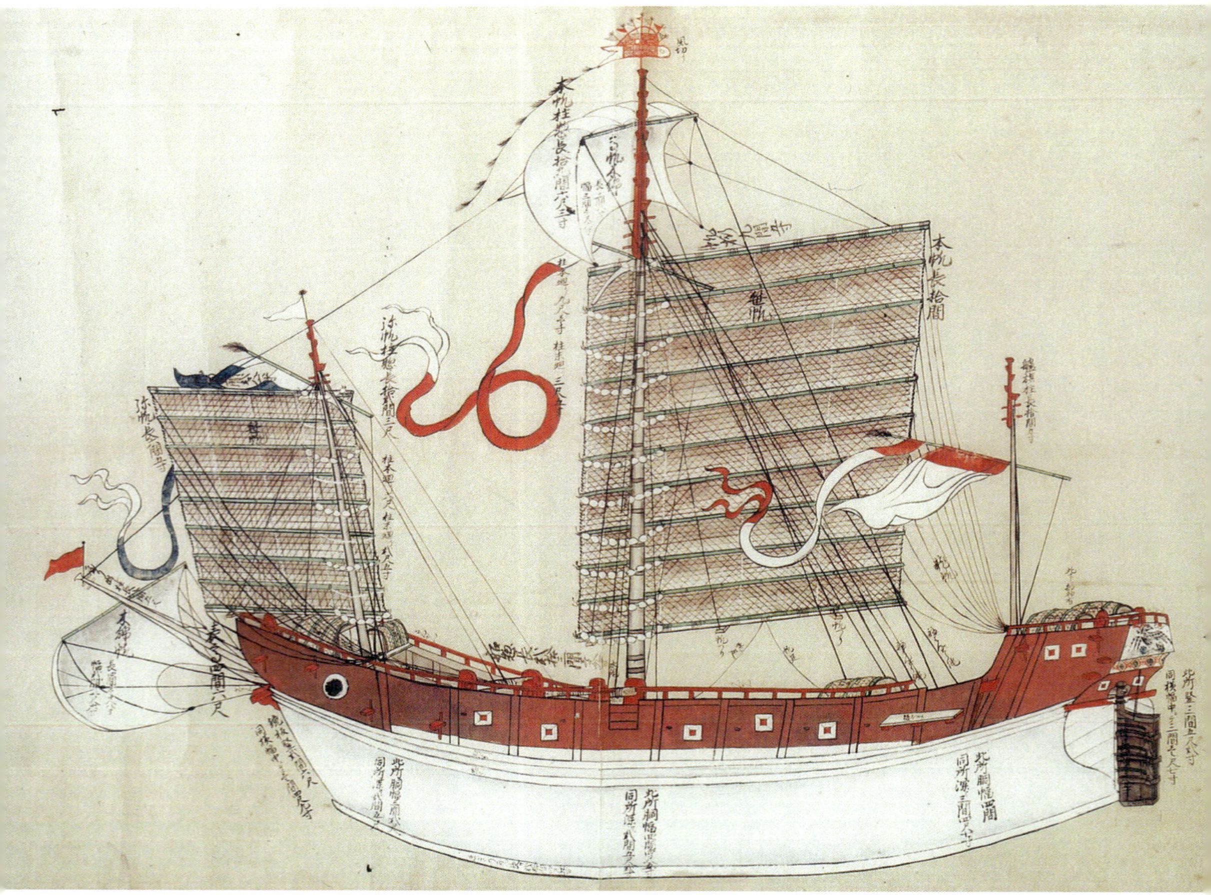

⊙ A Siamese ship owned by Fujian maritime merchants

⦿ A Guangdong ship made in Fuzhou

⦿ A Nanjing ship made in Fuzhou

⦿ A Nanjing ship

⦿ A Ningbo ship sailing to Nagasaki for trade

1.3 Ryukyu Ships

In the early Ming Dynasty, Ryukyu was a country with a poor economy. As an island country as it was, its navigation power was rather weak, and it was incapable of foreign transportation and trade activities. Since the establishment of the suzerain-vassal relationship with the Ming Dynasty, the Fujian Bureau for Foreign Shipping took charge of the trade and foreign affairs of Ryukyu. Thereinafter, Fujian became the shipbuilding base of Ryukyu. According to historical records, Ryukyu paid tributes to the emperor with ships, which were similar to Fuzhou ships. And the support from the Fujian shipbuilding industry helped Ryukyu's maritime power develop rapidly and the country developed a thriving maritime trade.

⊙ Ryukyu tribute ship in the 19th century, in the type of Fu ships, collected by the Okinawa County Museum, Japan

The hull of a Ming Dynasty Fu ship restored by the China Maritime Museum

The divine beast ornament at the prow of a Ming Dynasty Fu ship restored by the China Maritime Museum

The main deck and sails of a Ming Dynasty Fu ship restored by China Maritime Museum

The main and secondary masts on the deck of a Ming Dynasty Fu ship restored by the China Maritime Museum

⦿ The tail ornament of a Ming Dynasty Fu ship restored by the China Maritime Museum

⦿ The front deck of a Ming Dynasty Fu ship restored by China Maritime Museum

⦿ Intangible cultural heritage of Fujian Province – restoration of ancient ship model by ship construction technology in the Dongshan sea

⦿ The main building on the back deck of a Ming Dynasty Fu ship restored by the China Maritime Museum

2 Clamoring Harbors

The main ports of maritime trade between Fujian and Northeast Asia were the Fuzhou port, the Quanzhou port, the Moon Port of Zhangzhou, and the Taiwan ports. The Japanese ports that Fujian maritime merchants traded with were the Fukuoka Hakata-kō port, those at Gotō Islands, the Bōnotsu port in the south of Kagoshima, and the Nagasaki port, which later became the only open port in Japan during the period of self-seclusion. There were also ports in active trade with Fujian.

2.1 A Glimpse of Fujian's Trade Ports

Before the middle of the Ming Dynasty, the main ports of Fujian's maritime trade with Japan were the Moon Port of Zhangzhou and the Quanzhou port. In the middle and late Ming Dynasty, the Fuzhou port and the Dayuan port (i.e., Taiwan and Penghu) were the major trading venues.

The Moon Port, also known as Moon Spring Port, is 25 kilometers southeast of Zhangzhou city.

⊙ The Moon Port, Zhangzhou (today)

At the beginning of the Ming Dynasty, all Fujianese set out their sea trades from the Moon Port. In the first year of the Longqing period (1567), Emperor Muzong of the Ming Dynasty lifted the ban on maritime trade or intercourse with foreign countries, which gave the way for trade at the Moon Port to flourish.

By the Northern Song Dynasty, the Quanzhou port had opened routes to Goryeo and Japan. During the Yuanyou period (1086–1094) of the Northern Song Dynasty, Quanzhou merchant Xu Jian took Goryeo envoy Shou Jie and his entourage by ship to Hangzhou to build friendly foreign relations. Later, as there was no ship in Mingzhou to go to Goryeo when he began the journey back home, he travelled to Quanzhou for the return voyage.

During the Song and Yuan Dynasties, Fujian maritime merchants set out to Japan for trade as well. During the Chongning period (1102–1106) of the Northern Song Dynasty, Quanzhou maritime merchants sailed to Japan numerous times for trade. Judging from all kinds of Song Dynasty porcelain unearthed in Japan, many of them are comb-patterned celadon from Dehua kilns of Fujian, such as Kendis, boxes, goblets, and others. Archaeological findings also prove there was frequent communication between Fujian and Japan in the Song and Yuan Dynasties. By the Ming Dynasty, Quanzhou port had grown into one of the major ports of smuggling between China and Japan.

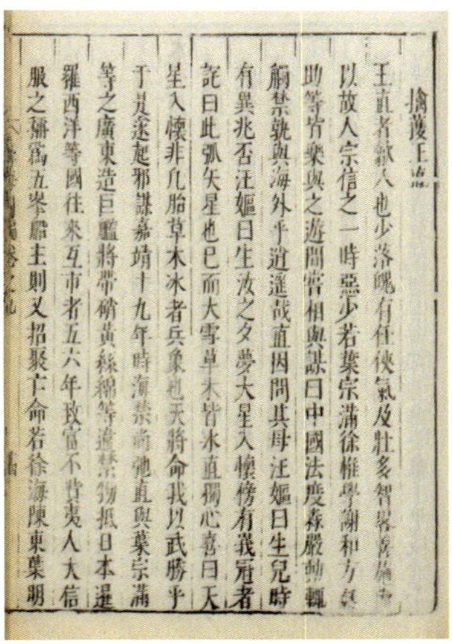

擒獲王直
王直者歙人也少落魄有任俠氣及壯多智略善施予
以故人宗信之一時惡少若葉宗滿徐惟學謝和方廷
助等皆樂與之遊間嘗相與謀曰中國法度森嚴動輒
觸禁孰與海外乎逍遙哉直因問其母汪嫗曰生兒時
有異兆否汪嫗曰生汝之夕夢大星入懷傍有峩冠者
詫曰此弧矢星也已而大雪草木皆冰直獨心喜曰天
星入懷非凡胎草木冰者兵象也天將命我以武勝乎
于是遂起邪謀嘉靖十九年時海禁尚弛直與葉宗滿
等之廣東造巨艦將帶硝黃絲綿等違禁物抵日本暹
羅西洋等國往來互市者五六年致富不貲夷人大信
服之稱爲五峯船主則又招聚亡命若徐海陳東葉明

Records of Ye Zongman and Xie He from Zhangzhou colluding with Wang Zhi to smuggle through the Moon Port and the Shuangyu port in the *Chou Hai Tu Bian*

⊙ Anping bridge in Quanzhou

⊙ Luoyang Bridge in Quanzhou

⊙ Liusheng pagoda in Shihu village, Shishi, Fujian, known as the first tower of Fujian Maritime Silk Road

⊙ The navigation mark of ancient Quanzhou port—Gusao pagoda

In 202 BC, present-day Fuzhou was Yecheng, the capital of Min. From there, the civilization history of the Fuzhou Port began.

In the Song Dynasty, Fuzhou became a pivotal place of imperial examinations, culture, and education, and an important base of Confucianism. The development of Fuzhou Port's overseas traffic promoted the development of its society and economy and the prosperity of its overseas trade.

⦿ Boats at the Min River Estuary

⦿ Wanshou bridge in Min River, Fuzhou and its downstream wooden boats (old scene)

2.2 Thriving Japanese Trade Ports

Fujian merchants mainly sailed to the west coast of Kyushu in Japan, such as Fukuoka Hakata-kō port, those on the Gotō Islands, Bōnotsu port in the south of Kagoshima in the early stage, and Nagasaki port in the middle and late stages.

Located off the west coast of Kyushu, the Gotō Islands were the only passage to Japan since ancient times. In both Fukuejima Island and Narushima Island, there are historical sites of Sino-Japanese trade exchanges.

There are the historical sites of Chinatown, the Hall of the Ming People, and the Hexagon Well on Fukuejima Island. Wang Zhi, Li Dan, and Zheng Zhilong used to reside on the island as they travelled between the coasts of China and Japan.

⊙ The Hall of the Ming People on Fukuejima Island, Japan

⦿ Commentary of the Hexagonal Well on Fukuejima Island, Japan

⦿ The Hexagonal Well on Fukuejima Island, Japan

⦿ Overlooking Fukuejima Bay, Japan

⦿ Yamagawa Bay, Kagoshima, Japan

⦿ Kagoshima Bōnotsu port in ancient Japanese Illustrated books

⦿ Kagoshima Bōnotsu port, Yamagawa port and the Gotō Islands depicted in *Treatise on Armament Technology or Records of Armaments and Military Provisions* (Japanese name: *Bubishi*)

Bōnotsu, a port in the south of Kagoshima Prefecture, used to be one of the strongholds for ships to send Japanese envoys to Tang China and Ming China, for Japanese pirate ships, and for Chinese private smuggling ships across the East China Sea. It was also one of the three big ports mentioned in Mao Yuanyi's Bubishi.

⦿ A bird's-eye view of Yamagawa port in Kagoshima, Japan, which used to be the designated port for Fujian goods to be transported to Satsuma by Ryukyu tribute ships

In the Ming and Qing Dynasties, Ryukyu became an intermediary force to connect the trade between China and Japan via entrepot trade in the name of tributary trade between China and Ryukyu and earned commercial benefits from it. In addition to Ryukyu ships, there were merchant ships from China, Southeast Asia, and western colonialists coming for trade. Yamakawa port retains the remains of the old Chinatown and Ishigantō stele of the Muromachi Shogunate Period (1336–1573).

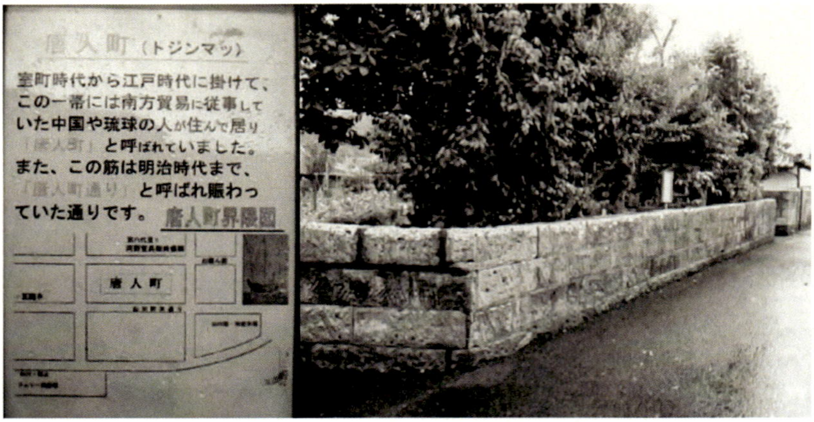

⦿ Remains of old Chinatown in Yamagawamachi, Kagoshima, Japan (old photo)

⦿ The old Chinatown streets of today in Yamagamamachi, Kagoshima, Japan

⦿ Ishigantō Stele

One more contribution of the Chinese merchants is the pickled radish stem, which is handed down from Fujian merchants. The local name is Yamagawatsuke or Tang-tsuke. Now it is one of the four major pickles in Japanese tradition.

The foreign trade of Hakata-kō port flourished in the 12th–13th centuries, during the Song and Yuan Dynasties in China. In the 14th century, as the Yuan army invaded Japan, and foreign trade was in recession during the war. From the 15th century to the 16th, it remained the beginning spot for the tribute trade between the Muromachi Shogunate and the Ming Dynasty. Ships sent to Ming China took off from Hakata-kō port to Ningbo via Hirado and the Gotō Islands. These trades introduced a great deal of Chinese goods into Hakata. Even now, many Chinese ceramics and copper coins in Hakata are still being discovered. In the 16th century, as the tribute trade in Japan and Ming Dynasty ended, the smuggling of Chinese maritime merchants expanded and the foreign trade stronghold moved to Hirado, Nagasaki, and Satsuma. In the early 17th century, Japan's overseas trade was limited to Nagasaki port, which was the end of Hakata-kō port being an overseas trade spot.

⦿ Map of Hakata-kō port in the early 17th century, collected by the Fukuoka Museum, Japan

⦿ Poster of the 500 years of making Yamakawatsuke (pickled radish)

Located in the coastal area in the middle of Osaka Prefecture, Japan, the city of Sakai, where Sakai port is situated, happened to be the juncture of Settsu Province, Kawachi Province, and Izumi Province during the Warring States period. Inland merchants of the three provinces gathered there to exchange goods with waterway merchants, allowing it to become a commercial port city. It was the spot where the anchors of Japanese ships set sails in 1469, 1476, 1483, 1506, and 1520. It was also the principal port for the smuggling of Ryukyu merchant ships and Portuguese merchant ships in the 16th century.

⦿ Nanban screens, collected by the Museum of Sakai City, Japan

3 The Endless Sea

In the Ming Dynasty, all foreign business people paid tribute with the guidance of the Bureau of Foreign Shipping. Especially subsequent to Zheng He's voyages to the west, the trade and transportation network between Fujian and Japan, the Korean Peninsula, and Southeast Asian countries gradually came into operation.

The first is the opening of the Sino-Ryukyu route. On the basis of previous navigation, the routes from Fujian to Ryukyu and from Fuzhou to Ryukyu have been documented in the two nautical guide manuals, *Shun Feng Xiang Song* and *Zhi Nan Zheng Fa*. Following the navigation guide from Ryukyu to Japan, there is a complete navigation route from Fujian to Japanese ports.

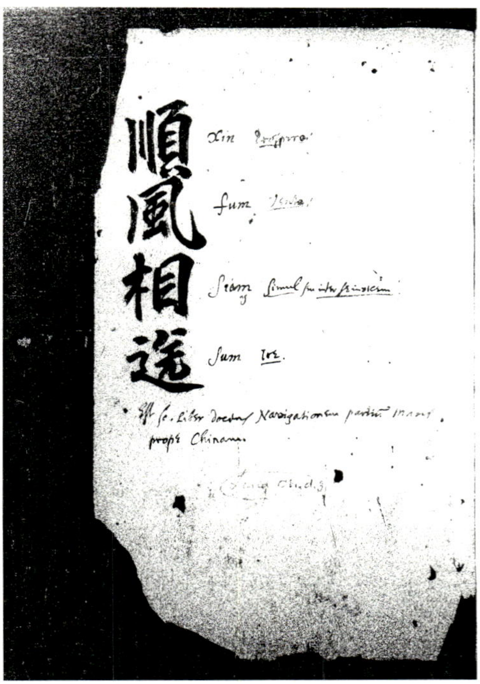

⦿ *Shun Feng Xiang Song*, sample page

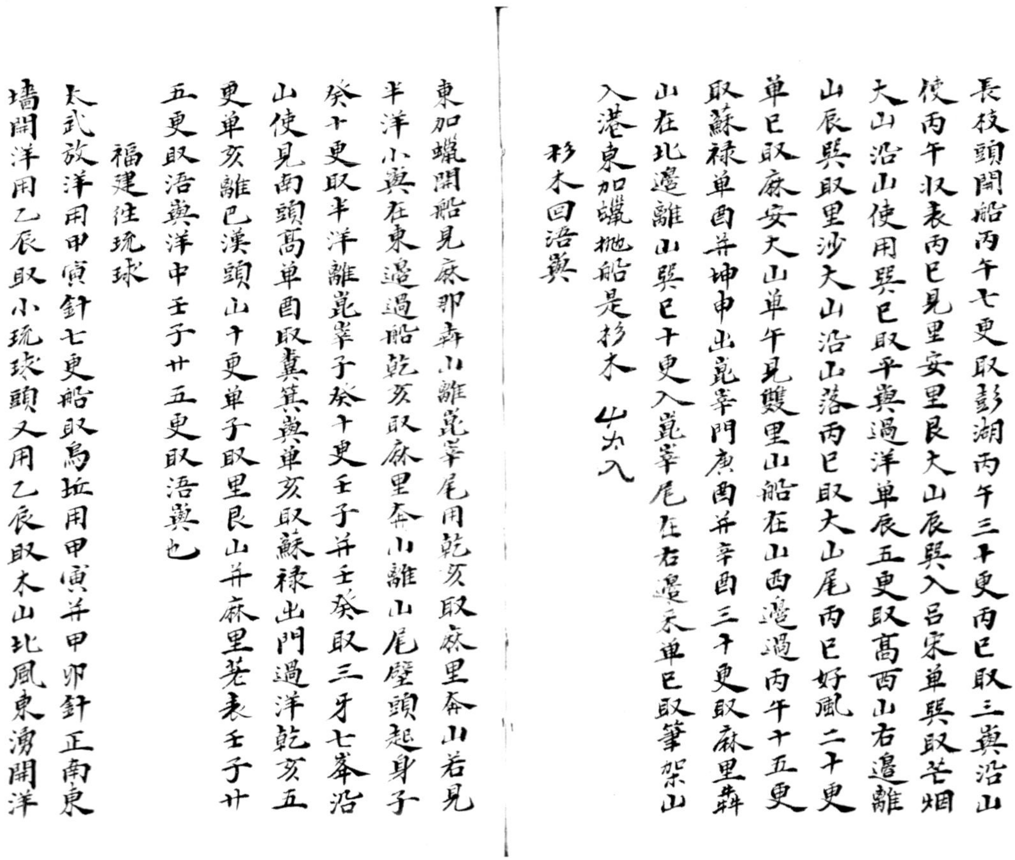
長枝頭開船丙午七更取彭湖丙午三十更丙巳取三嶼沿山
使丙午収表丙巳見里安里艮大山辰巽入呂宋单巽取芒烟
大山沿山使用巽巳取平嶼過洋单辰五更取高西山右邊離
山辰巽取里沙大山沿山落丙巳取大山尾丙巳好風二十更
单巳取麻安大山单午見雙里山船在山西邊過丙午十五更
取蘇祿单酉并坤申出崑崒門庚酉并辛酉三十更取麻里犇
山在北邊離山巽巳十更入崑崒尾在右邊不单巳取筆架山
入港東加蠟拋船是杉木 杉木入
杉木回浯嶼

東加蠟開船見麻那犇山離崑崒尾用乾亥取麻里奔山若見
半洋小嶼在東邊過船乾亥取麻里奔山離山尾壁頭起身子
癸十更取半洋離崑崒子癸十更壬子并壬癸取三牙七峯沿
山使見南頭高单酉取寘箕嶼单亥取蘇祿出門過洋乾亥五
更单亥離巴漢頭山十更单子取里艮山并麻里荖表壬子廿
五更取浯嶼洋中壬子廿五更取浯嶼也
福建往琉球
太武放洋用甲寅針七更船取烏坵用甲寅并甲卯針正南東
墻開洋用乙辰取小琉球頭又用乙辰取木山北風東湧開洋

⦿ Records on the sea route from Fujian to Ryukyu

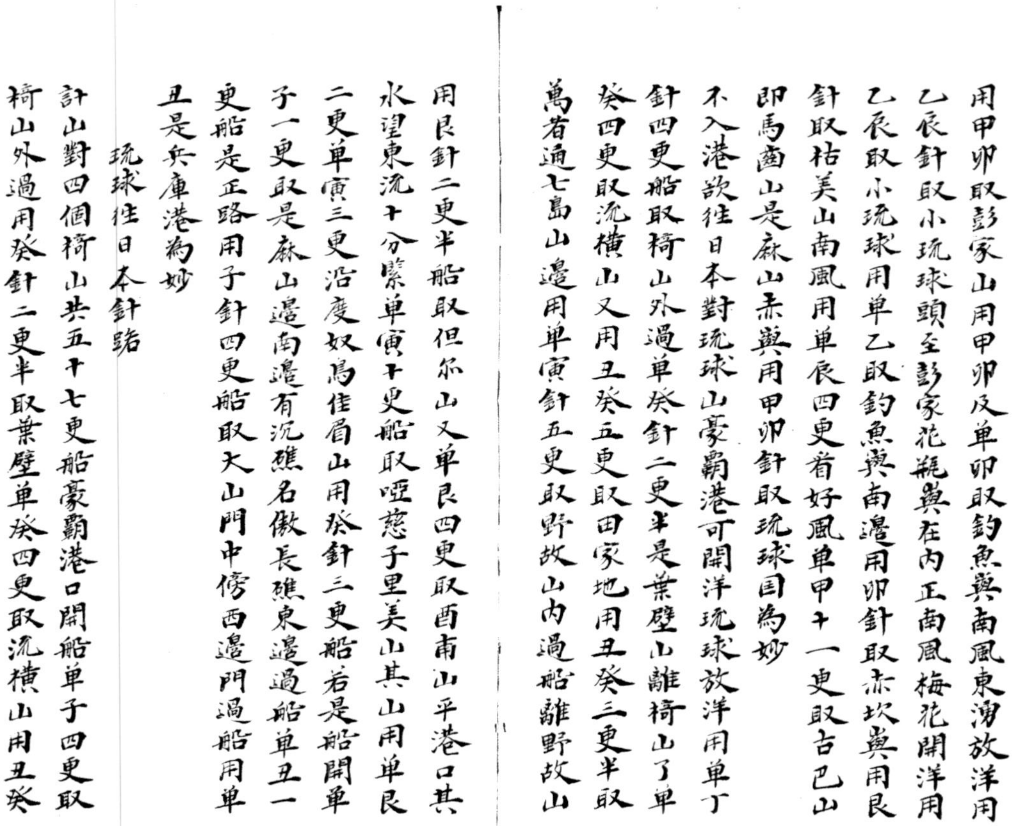

用甲卯取彭家山用甲卯及单卯取釣魚嶼南風東湧放洋用
乙辰取小琉球頭至彭家花瓶嶼在内正南風梅花開洋用
乙辰取小琉球用单乙取釣魚嶼南邊用卯針取赤坎嶼用艮
針取枯美山南風用单辰四更看好風单甲十一更取古巴山
即馬齒山是麻山赤嶼用甲卯針取琉球国為妙
不入港欲往日本對琉球山豪霸港可開洋琉球放洋用单丁
針四更船取椅山外過单癸針二更半是葉壁山離椅山了单
癸四更取流横山又用丑癸五更取田家地用丑癸三更半取
萬者通七島山邊用单寅針五更取野故山内過船離野故山
用艮針二更半船取但尔山又单艮四更取酉南山平港口其
水望東流十分緊单寅十更船取啞慈子里美山其山用单艮
二更单寅三更沿度奴烏佳眉山用癸針三更船若是船開单
子一更取是麻山邊南邊有沉礁名傲長礁東邊過船单丑一
更船是正路用子針四更船取大山門中傍西邊門過船用单
丑是兵庫港為妙

琉球往日本針路

計山對四個椅山共五十七更船豪霸港口開船单子四更取
椅山外過用癸針二更半取葉壁单癸四更取流横山用丑癸

⦿ Records of the sea route from Ryukyu to Japan

五更取田家地山用丑癸三更半取夢加利山単癸三更取大
羅山単癸二更半取萬者遖七垃山邊過単寅五更取野故山
内過艮針二更半取但尓山又艮針四更取野角利山平港口
流水望東十分急離野里山単寅十更取啞慈子里美山妙佳
眉山単癸三更若是船開単子一更取而麻山邊一個沉礁名
做長礁東邊過船単丑十更船是正路子針三更取大山門中
傍西邊門過船単丑三更取兵庫港為妙

兵庫港回琉球針路

港口開船単未三更単午四更取大門山中傍西邊過用午四
更取麻山単丁三更取沿渡奴烏佳眉山単辛針取啞慈子里
美山其山用辛針十一更取啞甫利山単坤六更取但尓山坤
申四更取野故山坤申五更取萬者遖七島山内過山名曰垃
奴名山共野山對向一更船有小礁五更船千萬仔細使船在
北邊過単丁三更取大羅山丁未三更取夢加利山用丁未五
更取葉壁山外過単丁三更取馬蹄山単午四更取琉球港口
為妙

琉球回福建

港口用坤申一更半平古已山是麻山用辛酉四更半用辰戌

⦿ Records of the route of returning to Ryukyu from Hyōgo port

In addition, *Zhi Nan Zheng Fa* also documents the round sea routes between Fuzhou and Ryukyu.

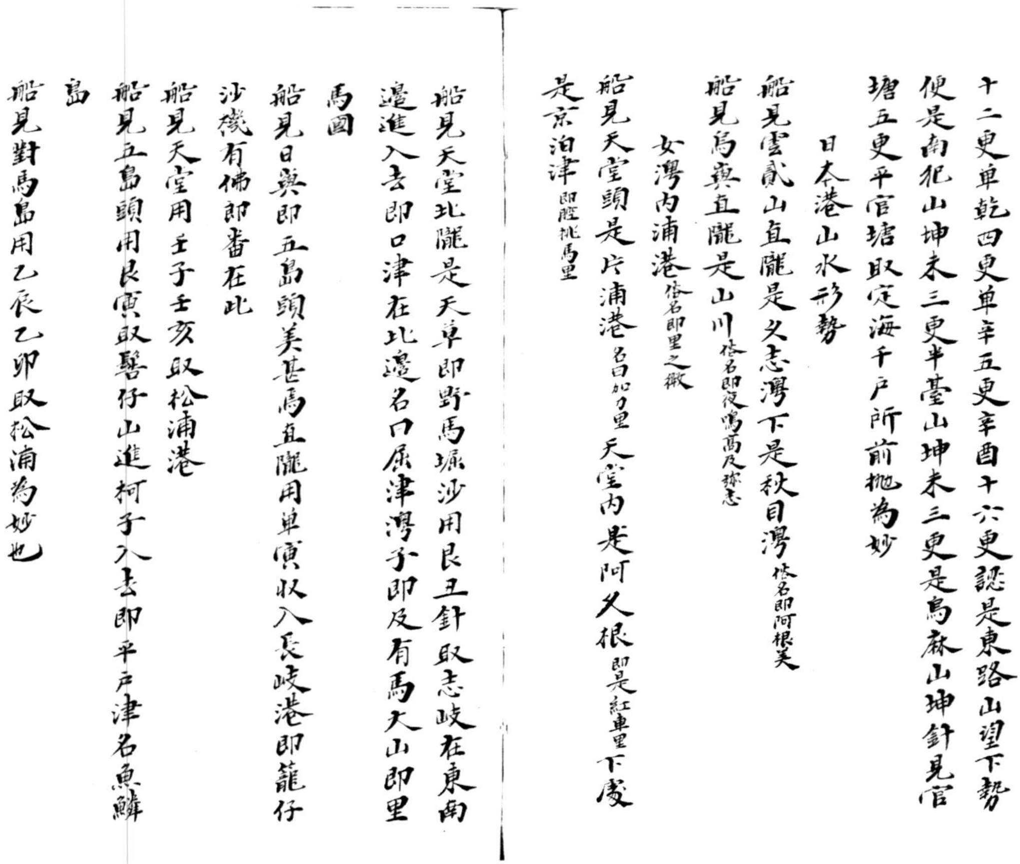

十二更單乾四更單辛五更辛酉十六更認是東路山望下勢
使是南杞山坤未三更半臺山坤未三更是烏麻山坤針見官
塘五更平官塘取定海千戶所前拋為妙

日本港山水形勢

船見雲貳山直隴是久志灣下是秋目灣倭名即阿根美
船見烏奐直隴是山川倭名即夜鳴高及捺志
女灣內浦港倭名即里之徹
船見天堂頭是片浦港名曰加乃里天堂內是阿久根即是紅東里下處
是京泊津即腔桃馬里

船見天堂北隴是天草即對馬塀沙用艮丑針取志岐在東南
邊進入去即口津在北邊名口原津灣予即及有馬大山即里
馬國
船見日奐即五島頭美甚高直隴用單寅收入長岐港即籠仔
沙機有佛郎番在此
船見天堂用壬子壬亥取松浦港
船見五島頭用艮寅取磬仔山進柯子入去即平戶津名魚鱗
島
船見對馬島用乙辰乙卯取松浦為妙也

⦿ Records of the return sea route from Ryukyu to Fujian

In addition to the records of navigational charts, the dialogues between the envoys who were sent to Ryukyu and the boatmen recorded the sea routes between Fujian and the Northeast Asian countries, which were presented in the form of nautical charts. For example, during the reign of Emperor Kangxi of the Qing Dynasty (1662–1722), the nautical chart made on the basis of the envoy Xu Baoguang's voyage to Ryukyu made a clear depiction of the sea route from Fujian to Northeast Asia.

In ancient times, there were many forms of sea route presentation in China. In addition to the two forms mentioned above, there was one that was more straightforward, the mountain-water-chart. It presented both pictures and texts, thus practical for those who were used to sailing but could not read much.

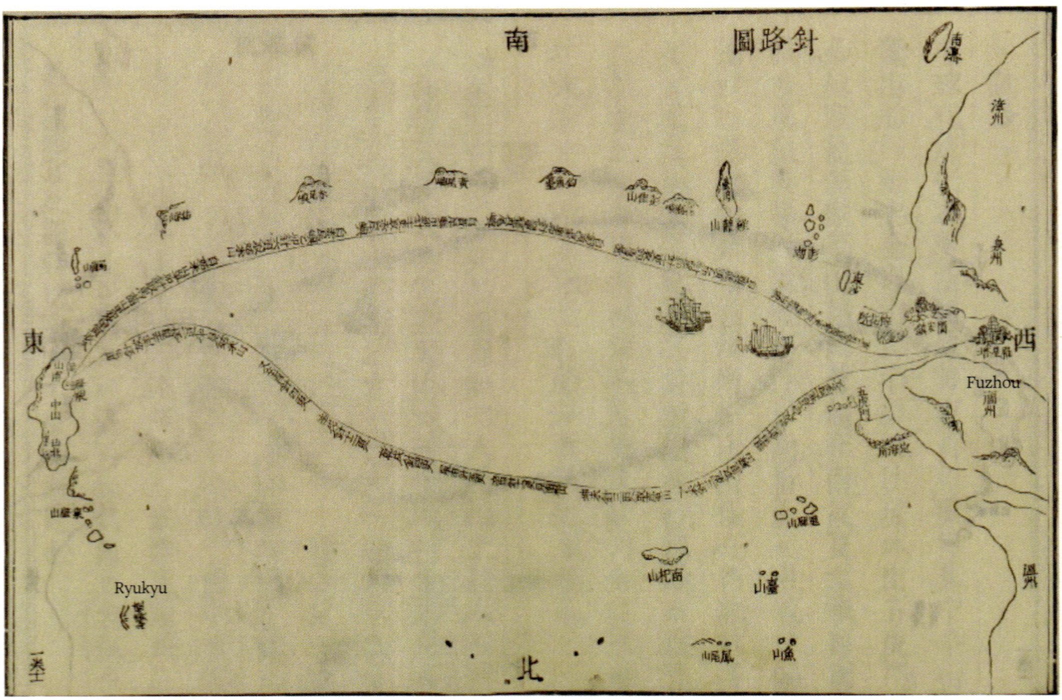

⦿ Nautical chart made on the basis of the envoy Xu Baoguang's voyage to Ryukyu

⦿ Mountain-water-map of ancient navigation

The ancient nautical charts enable us to have a better understanding of the ancient navigational routes, such as the *Nautical Charts of the Imperial Envoys to Ryukyu* drawn by Zhu Henian in the Qianlong period of the Qing Dynasty (1736–1795).

⦿ Part of the *Passing the Strait at Midnight* in the *Nautical Charts of the Imperial Envoys to Ryukyu*

CHAPTER 5

THE MINGLING OF COMMERCE AND CULTURE

In ancient times, the communication between Fujian and neighboring Japan was commercial primarily trade, which inevitably involved cultural exchanges and integration of many aspects, including ideas, systems, customs, education, religion, and production skills.

1 Various Trade Goods

There were two major forms of trade between Fujian and Japan in the Ming Dynasty. One was the early tally trade, and the other was the smuggling dominated by Fujian maritime merchants in the middle and later periods. During the period of Muromachi Shogunate (1336–1573), the separatist regime and constant civil war of Japan negatively affected its domestic production. Moreover, the handicraft industry, which had been newly separated from agriculture, was rather underdeveloped. The currency and various necessities of life, such as silk, cloth, pots, needles, and medicinal materials in the Japanese market, were supplied by China.

1.1 Cash and Goods in Great Demand in the Japanese Market

The rally trade enabled Japan to import a large amount of copper cash from China to finance the market circulation. For example, Hongwu Tongbao and Yongle Tongbao were once the hard currencies in the domestic market of Japan. Most of the copper cash was transported to Japan by Fujian and Zhejiang merchants or Zheng Chenggong's merchant ships.

⦿ Hongwu Tongbao

⊙ Yongle Tongbao

⊙ Longwu Tongbao

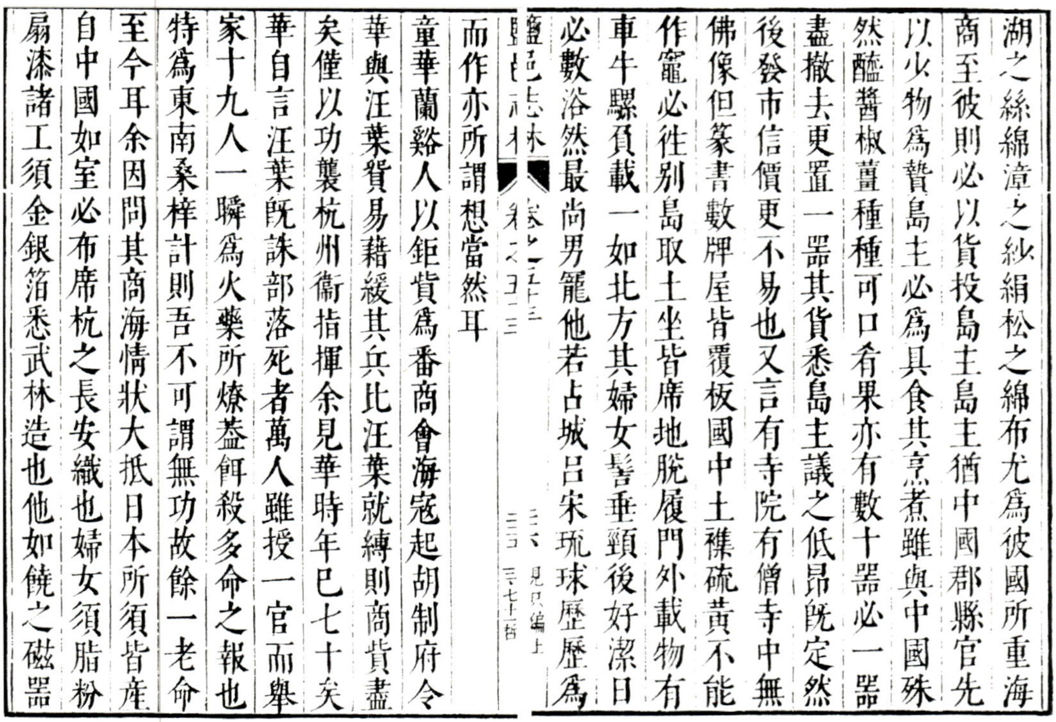

湖之絲綿漳之紗絹松之綿布尤爲彼國所重海
商至彼則必以貨投島主島主循中國郡縣官先
以火物爲贄島主必爲具食其烹煮雖與中國殊
然醯醬椒薑種種可口肴果亦有數十器必一器
盡撤去更置一器其貨悉島主議之低昂既定然
後發市信價更不易也又言有寺院有僧寺中無
佛像但篆書數牌屋皆覆板國中土襍硫黃不能
作竈必往別島取土坐皆席地脫履門外載物有
車牛騾負載一如北方其婦女髻垂頸後好潔日
必數浴然最尚男寵他若占城呂宋琉球歷歷爲
而作亦所謂想當然耳
童華蘭谿人以鉅貲爲番商會海寇起胡制府令
華與汪葉貿易藉緩其兵比汪葉就縛則商貲盡
矣僅以功襲杭州衛指揮余見華時年已七十矣
華自言汪葉既誅部落死者萬人雖授一官而舉
家十九人一瞬爲火藥所燎蓋餌殺多命之報也
特爲東南桑梓計則吾不可謂無功故餘一老命
至今耳余因問其商海情狀大抵日本所須皆產
自中國如室必布席杭之長安織也婦女須脂粉
扇漆諸工須金銀箔悉武林造也他如饒之磁器

⊙ The records of a large number of daily necessities transported to Japan from the Yangtze River Valley and southeast coast in the middle of Ming Dynasty in *Jian Zhi Bian*

During the Jiajing reign (1522–1566) of the Ming Dynasty, *Chou Hai Tu Bian*, a large-scale military treatise, compiled by Zheng Ruozeng, et al., recorded the Chinese goods badly needed in Japan at that time.

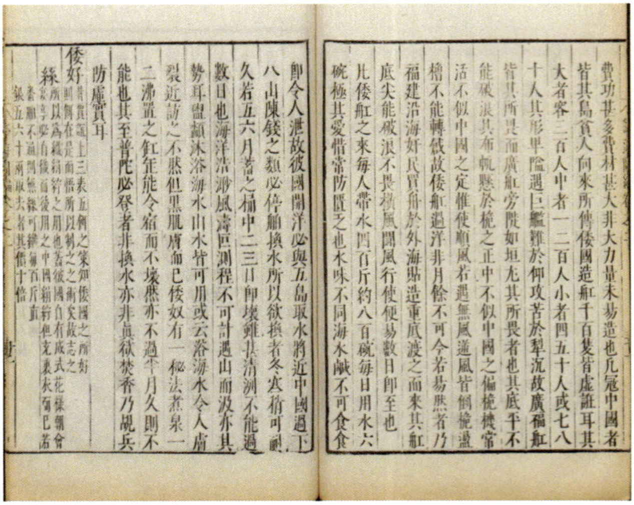

費功甚多或材甚大非大力量未易造也凡寇中國者
皆其島貧人向來所傳倭國造舡千百隻皆虛誑耳其
大者容三百人中者一二百人小者四五十人或七八
十人其形卑隘遇巨艦難於仰攻苦於犁沉故廣福舡
皆其所畏而廣舡旁陡如垣尤其所畏者也其底平不
能破浪其布帆懸於桅之正中不似中國之偏桅檣常
活不似中國之定惟使順風若遇無風逆風皆倒桅盪
櫓不能轉戧故倭舡過洋非月餘不可今若易然者乃
福建沿海奸民買舟於外海貼造重底渡之而來其舡
底尖能破浪不畏橫風鬭風行使便易數日即至也
凡倭舡之來每人帶水四百斤約八百碗每日用水六
碗極其愛惜常防匱乏也水味不同海水鹹不可食食

即令人泄故彼國開洋必與五島取水將近中國過下
八山陳錢之類必停船換水所以欲換者冬寒猶可耐
久若五六月蓄之桶中二三日即壞雖甚清洌不能過
數日也海洋浩渺風濤叵測程不可計遇山而汲亦其
勢耳豈顧沐浴海水山水皆可用或云浴海水令人膚
裂近訪之不然但黑肌膚而已倭奴有一秘法煮泉一
二沸置之缸年能令宿而不壞然亦不過半月久則不
能也其至普陀必登者非換水亦非真欲焚香乃覘兵
防虛實耳

倭好 賈誼上三表五餌之策知倭國之所好則餌在是而借所以制之之術矣故志之

絲 所以為織絹紵之用也蓋彼國自有成式花樣朝會宴享必自織而後用之中國絹紵但充裏衣而已若番舶不通則無絲可織每百斤直銀五六百兩取去者其價十倍

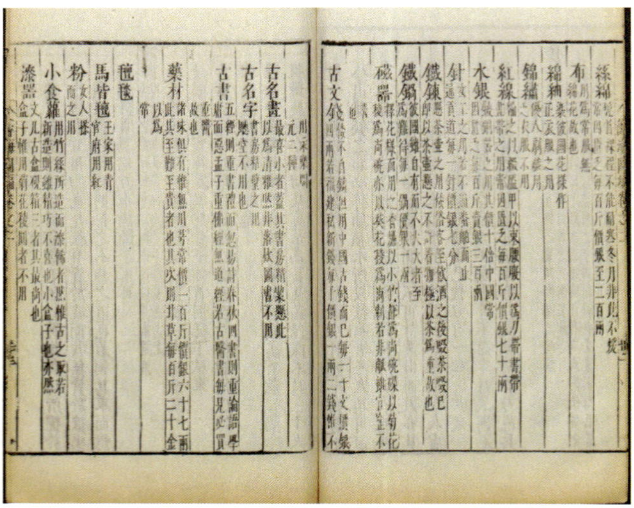

絲綿 髡首裸程不能耐寒冬月非此不煖常因匱乏每百斤價銀至二百兩

布 用為常服無綿花故也

綿紬 染彼國花樣作正衣服之用

錦繡 優人劇戲用衣服不用

紅線 編之以綴盔甲以束腰腹以為刀帶書帶畫帶之用常因匱乏每百斤價銀七十兩

水銀 鍍銅器之用其價十倍中國常因匱乏每百斤賣銀三百兩

針 女工之用若不通番舶而止通貢道每一針價銀七分

鐵鍊 懸茶壺之用倭俗客至飲酒之後啜茶啜已即以茶壺懸之不許着地極以茶為重故也

鐵鍋 彼國雖自有而不大大者至為難得每一鍋價銀一兩

磁器 擇花樣而用之香爐以小竹節為尚碗碟以菊花稜為尚碗亦以葵花稜為尚制若非觚雖官窯不喜也

古文錢 倭不自鑄但用中國古錢而已每一千文價銀四兩若福建私新錢每千價銀一兩二錢惟不用永樂開元二種

古名畫 最喜小者蓋其書房精潔懸此以為清雅然非落款圖書不用

古名字 書房粘壁之用廳堂不用也

古書 五經則重書禮而忽易詩春秋四書則重論語學庸而惡孟子重佛經無道經若古醫書每見必買重醫故也

藥材 諸味俱有惟無川芎常價一百斤價銀六十七兩其次則甘草每百斤二十金以為常

氈毯

馬背氈 王家用青官府用紅

粉 女人搽面之用

小食籮 用竹絲所造而漆飾者然惟古之取若新造則絲粗不巧不喜也小盒子亦然

漆器 文几古盒硯箱三者其最尚也盒子惟用菊花稜圓者不用

⦿ Records of Chinese goods widely appreciated by the Japanese in *Chou Hai Tu Bian*

⊙ Embroidered works from Zhangzhou

1.2 Massively Salable Fujian Porcelain in Japan

In the Tang and Song Dynasties, the ceramic manufacturing industry flourished. Under the promotion of the positive trade policy of the imperial court, ceramics became a major export commodity only second to silk. In the Song Dynasty, the white porcelain from Dehua kilns in Fujian Province, together with the celadon and bluish white porcelain from Yue Kilns and Longquan kilns, was exported globally, including the Korean Peninsula and Japan.

During the Yuan Dynasty, the scale of Chinese porcelain exports was unprecedented. In 1977, up to 18,000 pieces of Chinese porcelain were found on the Xin'an ship excavated in Mokpo City, South Korea, including many folk kiln products from Zhangzhou, Fujian Province.

Cizao kilns were important kilns making export ceramics in the Song and Yuan Dynasties. It is located in Cizao Town, Jinjiang, Fujian Province. Ceramics manufacturing there began in the late Southern Dynasty, flourished in the Song and Yuan Dynasties, and lasted until the Ming and Qing Dynasties.

⊙ At the Kōrokan site (Hakata, Fukuoka), where Song Dynasty envoys were received in Japan, southern Fujian ceramics were unearthed

During the Song and Yuan Dynasties, the products of Cizao kilns were exported to Japan and Southeast Asian countries.

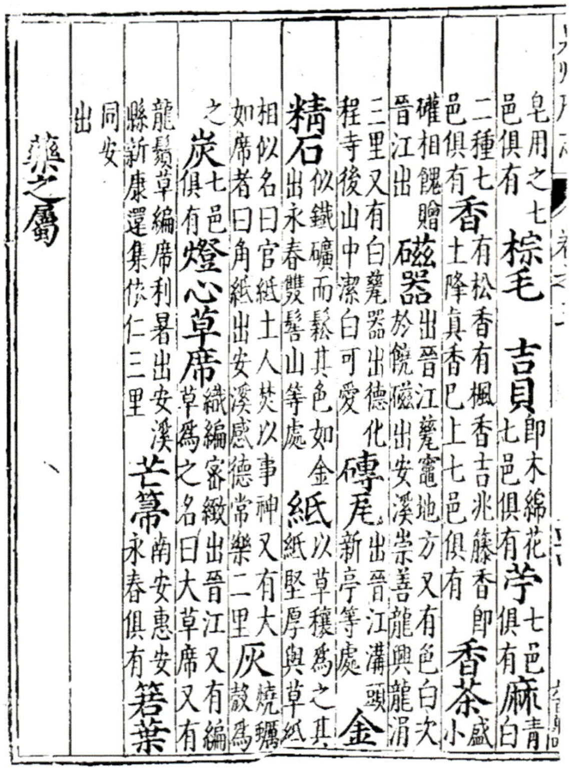

皂用之七邑俱有棕毛吉貝即木綿花七邑俱有苧七邑俱有麻青白
二種七邑俱有香有松香有楓香吉兆藤香即土降真香已上七邑俱有香茶盛小
確相饋贈晉江出磁器出晉江甆竈地方又有色白次於饒磁出安溪崇善龍興龍涓
三里又有白甆器出德化程寺後山中潔白可愛磚瓦出晉江溝頭新亭等處金
精石似鐵礦而鬆其色如金出永春雙髻山等處紙以草穰爲之其紙堅厚與草紙
相似名曰官紙土人焚以事神又有大如席者曰角紙出安溪感德常樂二里灰燒蠣殼爲
之炭七邑俱有燈心草席織編密緻出晉江又有編草爲之名曰大草席又有
龍鬚草編席利暑出安溪縣新康還集依仁三里芒箒南安惠安永春俱有箬葉
同安出
藤之屬

⦿ Restoration of the site of Cizao kilns in *Records of Quanzhou*, sample page

⦿ Yellow glazed ceramic pot from Cizao kilns unearthed in Japan

⦿ Yellow glazed ceramic bowl from Cizao kilns unearthed in Japan

From the end of the 16th century to the beginning of the 17th century, folk kilns in Zhangzhou, Fujian Province, and Chaoshan, Guangdong Province, were widely producing bright blue and white porcelains and overglazed enamels for daily use. Thanks to the rise of Fujian maritime merchants and the prosperity of the private maritime trade in the late Ming and early Qing Dynasties, these porcelains were gathered in the Moon Port, Zhangzhou, to be shipped all over the world along the road of maritime ceramics, most of which arrived in Japan. A large number of these porcelains have been excavated in modern times from historical sites in Japan, such as the Hataka site group, Osaka Castle site, Nagasaki site, and Hirado Dutch business hall site. They are called gosu-akae, Swatow wares, gosu-sometsuke, and mochibana-de by Japanese scholars and museum collectors.

⦿ Flowers in overglazed enamel plate produced by Zhangzhou kilns, collected in Japan

⦿ Figures in overglazed enamel plate produced by Zhangzhou kilns, collected in Japan

⦿ The celadon bowl produced from Zhangzhou kilns, collected in Japan

⦿ Flowers and birds in overglazed enamel plate produced by Zhangzhou kilns, collected in Japan

⊙ Overglazed enamels bowl produced by Zhangzhou kilns, collected in Japan

⊙ Overglazed little enamels produced by Zhangzhou kilns, collected in Japan

During this period, white porcelain Avalokitesvara (Guanyin) produced by the Dehua kilns and other Fujian kilns were purchased and collected by some Catholics in Kyushu, Japan. While the Japanese shogunate banned the spread of Catholicism among the Japanese people during the Ming and Qing Dynasties, they secretly worshipped the white porcelain Avalokitesvara as the Virgin Mary.

⊙ Trade porcelain produced by Zhangzhou kilns, unearthed in Osaka, Japan

⊙ Avalokitesvara, Goddess of Mercy

1.3 Jian Zhan (tea bowls) and Japan

Tea drinking and tea competitions gained popularity in Song Dynasty. And ceramic tea bowls were indispensable utensils. One of them was called black glazed tea bowl, whose color and technology were rather complementary to the tea itself and made it easy to observe the color of tea. It was widely loved as the best for a tea competition.

Jian Zhan, as the main utensil for drinking and competing tea at that time, was popular with literati and officials and favored by Buddhist monks in Fujian and Zhejiang. Famous temples and eminent monks attracted many Japanese monks to come to seek the Dharma. They brought back Buddhist scriptures and learned the custom of tea-tasting. When they returned to Japan, they carried a large number of black glazed tea bowls, including Jian Zhan. As soon as Jian Zhan entered Japanese society, it earned the appreciation of the upper class, monks, and samurai. It was regarded as a treasure by the tea ceremony circles and named *Tenmoku* in Japanese.

⦿ Tenmoku Jian Zhan, collected by Tōyō Ceramic Art Gallery, Osaka, Japan

⦿ Tenmoku Jian Zhan with golden characters, collected by Gōkō Fine Arts Gallery in Japan

⦿ Black glazed spotted tea bowl (Jian Kiln bowl or Tenmoku bowl), collected by Gōkō Fine Arts Gallery in Japan

⦿ Jian Kiln tea bowl (Tenmoku bowl), collected by Kyoto National Museum, Japan

The contingency in the process of firing ceramics led to an extremely special finished product in Jian Zhan, which is Yōhen Tenmoku. Its dreamy color and rarity have made it the best of the black glazed tea bowls.

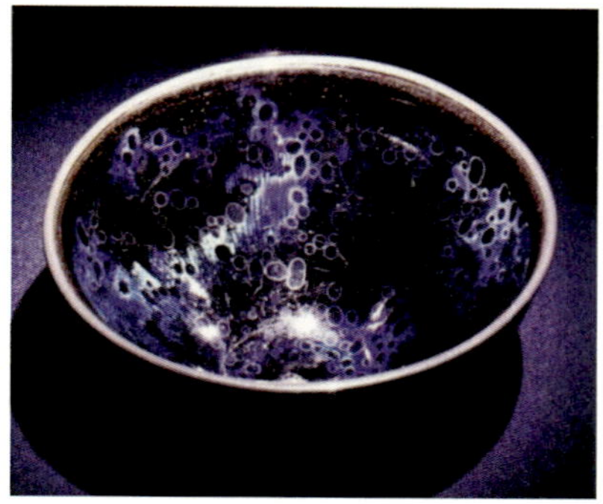

⊙ Black glazed Jian Zhan, Yōhen Tenmoku, collected by Seikadō Bunko Art Museum

⊙ Tenmoku Jian Zhan with golden characters, collected by Gōkō Fine Arts Gallery in Japan

⊙ Inside patterns of black glazed Jian Zhan, Yōhen Tenmoku, collected by Ryōkō-in of Daitoku-ji Temple, Japan

1.4 Japanese Pirate Swords and Carved Lacquer Folding Screens

In the Ming Dynasty, the constant frontier war in China greatly demanded the import of weapons. In the early Ming Dynasty, Japanese tribute ships and Fujian and Zhejiang merchant ships transported back a large number of Japanese swords through the tally trade. And their long history, excellent workmanship, and fine shape earned them a satisfactory market share in China.

⊙ Swords that Japan exported to China

⊙ Famous Japanese swords in the early period of Muromachi Shogunate

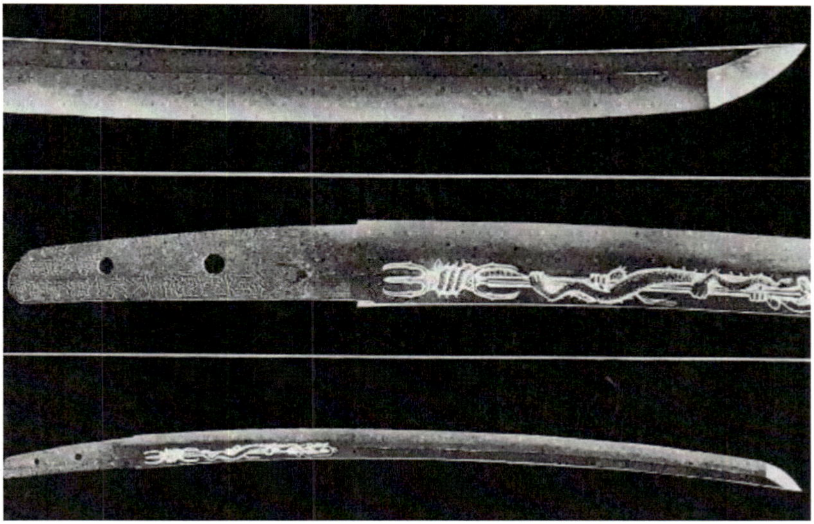

⊙ Famous Japanese swords in the middle period of the Muromachi Shogunate

⊙ Japanese pear blossom and chrysanthemum patterned Tachi sword, a high-quality broadsword, collected by the Palace Museum

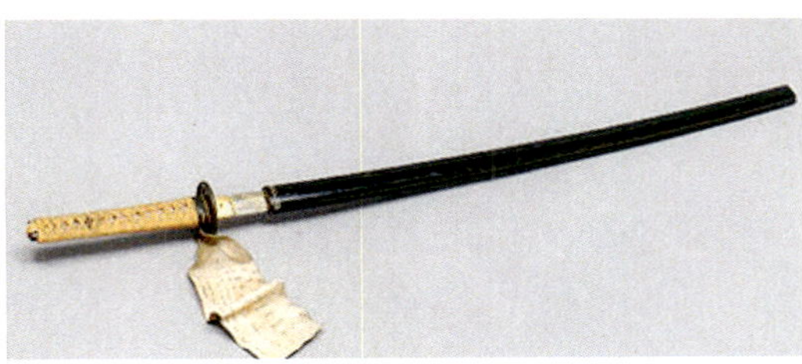

⊙ Ryukyu tribute sword, whose blade and edge were made in Japan, handle and sheath processed in Ryukyu, collected by the Palace Museum

In the maritime trade between Fujian and Japan, Japanese lacquerware products were imported into the Chinese market in large quantities, such as carved lacquer folding screens and illuminated paintings. Especially during the reign of Qianlong emperor of the Qing Dynasty, Emperor Qianlong adored the lacquerware of Japan and Ryukyu. He used to order the General of Fuzhou to buy it immediately. In this way, the maritime merchants imported a large number of lacquerware products from Japan and other countries and distributed them across mainland of China.

⦿ Palace guards, equipped with Japanese swords, of the Ming Dynasty, collected by the Palace Museum

⦿ Japanese folding screens purchased by Fujian and Zhejiang merchants in the Ming Dynasty (1)

⦿ Japanese folding screen painting in Muromachi Shogunate period – Portuguese business people travelling to Japan on Zheng Chenggong's merchant ship

⦿ The folding screen of flowers and birds, an important cultural relic of Japan. The same screens were presented to the emperor of the Ming Dynasty

⊙ Japanese folding screens purchased by Fujian and Zhejiang merchants in the Ming Dynasty (2)

⊙ Japanese lacquerware and illuminated paintings purchased by Fujian and Zhejiang merchants in the Ming Dynasty (1)

⊙ Japanese lacquerware and illuminated paintings purchased by Fujian and Zhejiang merchants in the Ming Dynasty (2)

2 Books and Woodblock Printing Technique

At the end of the Yuan Dynasty, a number of Chinese woodblock printing technicians escaped to Japan to survive the war. It happened that many Buddhist temples in the Kinki area of Kansai Prefecture of Japan were vigorously making copies of various Buddhist scriptures and quotations of eminent monks. Therefore, these Chinese woodblock printing technicians were employed for the woodblock printing projects of temples, and some raised funds among themselves to print collections of Chinese poems and essays. Statistics showed that there were more than 50 Chinese, mostly from Fujian and Zhejiang Provinces, who came to Japan and engaged in the printing of Buddhist scriptures. The most famous was Yu Liangfu, who came from Putian County, Xinghua Road, Fujian Province, and Chen Mengqian, Chen Boshou from Nantai bridge, Fuzhou City.

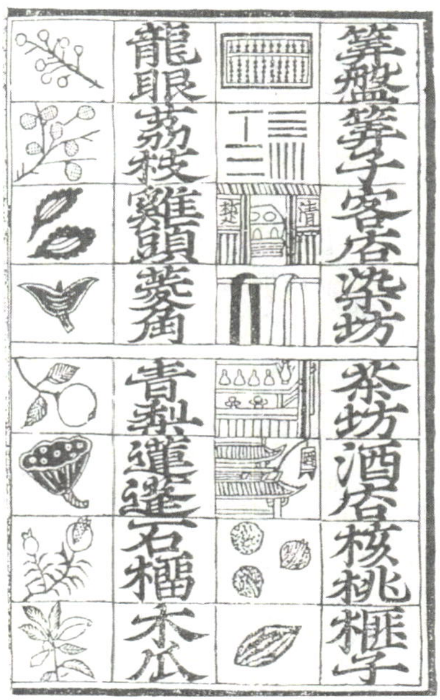

⦿ *Miscellaneous Characters of the Basic Four-words-in-couples*, printed by Chen Boshou, a woodblock printing technician of Fuzhou Nantai, and collected in Japan

2.1 Yu Liangfu, a woodblock printing technician who traveled to Japan

Yu Liangfu, a native of Yuli village, Xitianwei Town, Licheng District, Putian City, Fujian Province, sailed across the sea to Japan in 1367. During his residence in Saga, Tokyo, Yu typographed eight documents, including *the Quotations of Monk Tsukie, Shūgyōroku, Collection of Bishan Hall,* and the *Newly-published Anthology of Mr. Tang Liu with Five-Hundred Phonetic Notations*. In addition, he also raised funds to publish a variety of classics, such as *Shunjun Keiden Shikkai, A Collective Annotation of the Spring and Autumn Classics, Selected Works, Han Changli Anthology, Master Liu's Works from the Tang Dynasty*, and *The Well-selected Poetry of Lu Fang-weng*. He left a mark of himself on all the works he printed in Japan, "By Yu Liangfu of the Tang Dynasty" or "By Yu Liangfu, a resident of Rendeli, Putian, Xinghua Road, Fujian Province."

⦿ The tablet of Yu's family

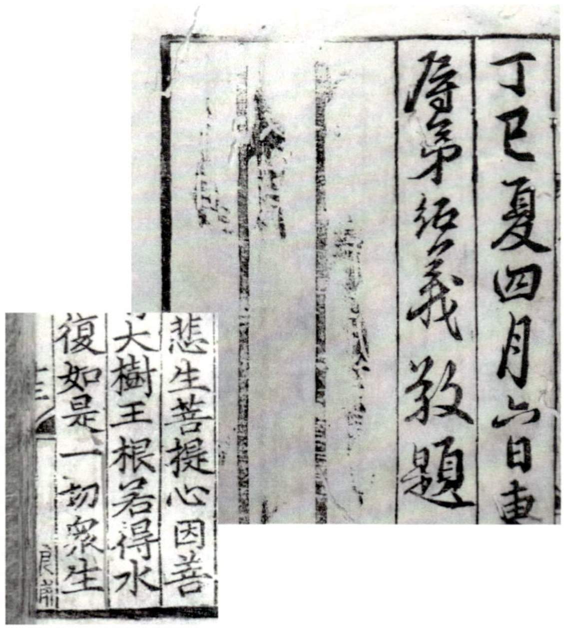

⦿ *Quotations of Monk Tsukie*, published in 1370 and printed by Yu Liangfu, collected by the Museum of History and Folklore

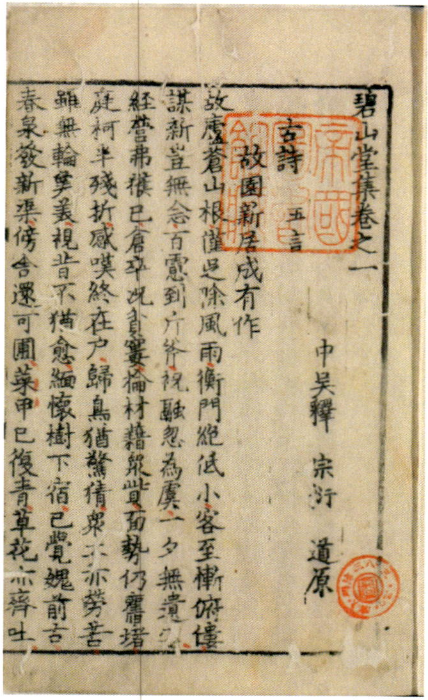

⊙ *Collection of Bishan Hall* (Northern and Southern Dynasties Edition), printed by Yu Liangfu, collected by the National Diet Library, Japan

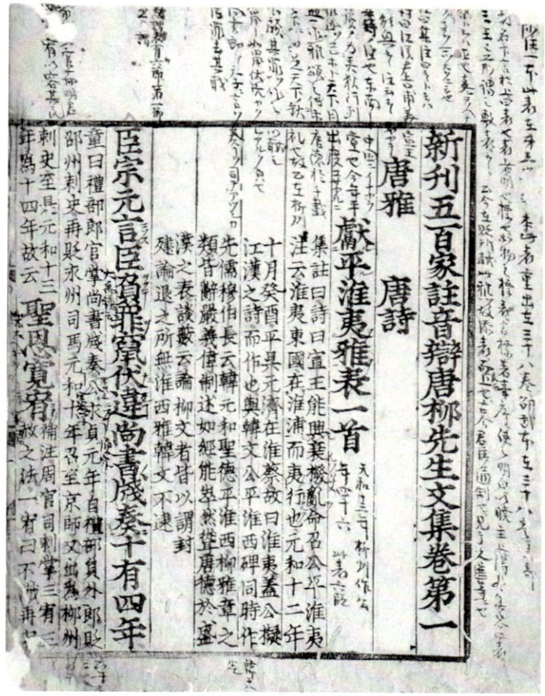

⊙ *Newly-published Anthology of Mr. Tang Liu with Five-Hundred Phonetic Notations*, printed by Yu Liangfu

Japanese scholars greatly admired Yu Liangfu's woodblock printing techniques, thus naming his work Yu Version. The Chinese woodblock printing technicians' printing of both Buddhist scriptures and works of famous literature of the Tang and Song Dynasties made great contributions to Japanese culture. Japanese scholar Kimiya Taiyan pointed out that their contributions to the development of Japanese culture would never be forgotten.

2.2 The Fujian Version of the Chinese Buddhist Canon Spread to Japan

The Buddhist scriptures printed in Fujian in Song Dynasty were introduced to Japan in large quantities, among which the Fuzhou version of the *Chinese Buddhist Canon* was the most outstanding. Since the introduction of Buddhism to China, the translation, copying, editing, woodcarving, printing, dissemination, and worship of Buddhist scriptures by monks have become a significant part of the development of Buddhism.

⦿ Hongan-ji Temple in Kyoto, Japan, possessing a collection of *The Chinese Buddhist Canon*, which was published by the Dongchan Temple in Fuzhou and other Zen temples in the Northern Song Dynasty

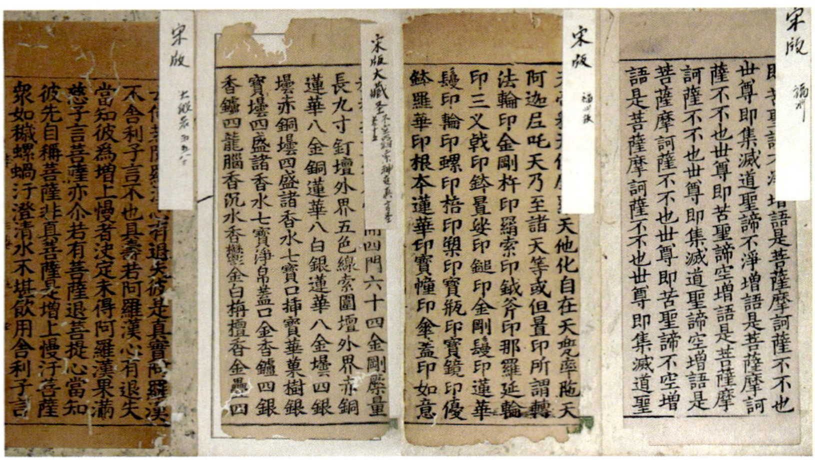

⦿ Song Dynasty version of *The Chinese Buddhist Canon* in Fuzhou, sample page, collected by the Hongan-ji Temple in Kyoto, Japan

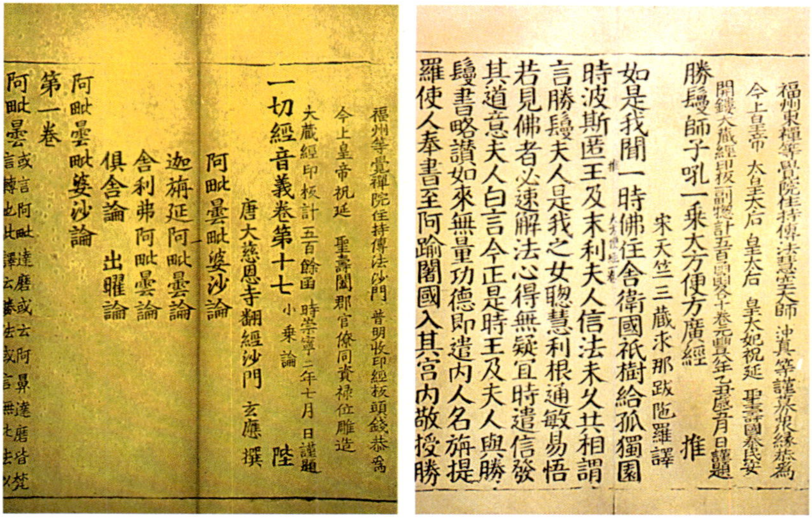

⦿ *The Chinese Buddhist Canon* published by Dongchan Temple in Fuzhou and other Zen temples in the Northern Song Dynasty and collected by the Hongan-ji Temple in Kyoto, Japan

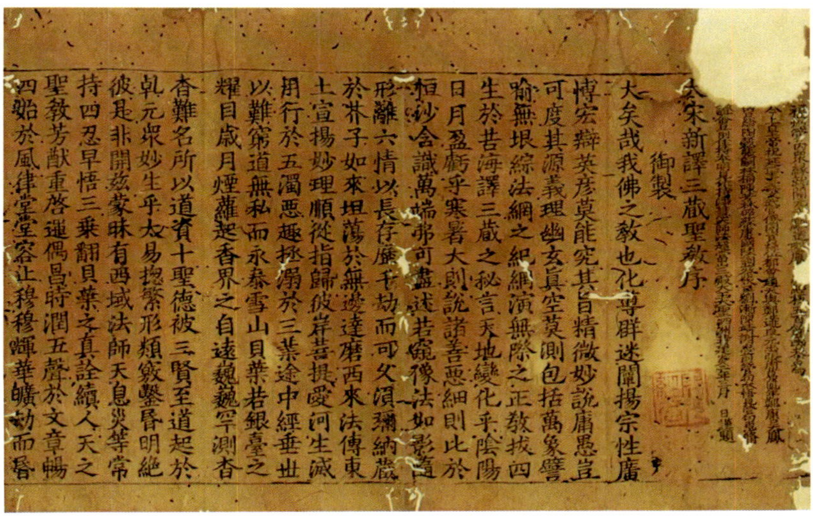

⦿ *Vairocana Buddhist Canon* of the Kaiyuan Temple in Fuzhou, sample page (1), collected by Waseda University, Japan

From 1112 to 115, the Kaiyuan Temple in Fuzhou also printed *The Vairocana Buddhist Canon of Kaiyuan Temple in Fuzhou*, also known as *The Vairocana Buddhist Canon*.

The two Chinese Buddhist canons mentioned above were imported into Japan by Japanese monks in the Song Dynasty and Chinese business people and became collections of famous temples and Japanese royal families and nobles. It had a significant impact on the dissemination and printing of Buddhist classics in Japan.

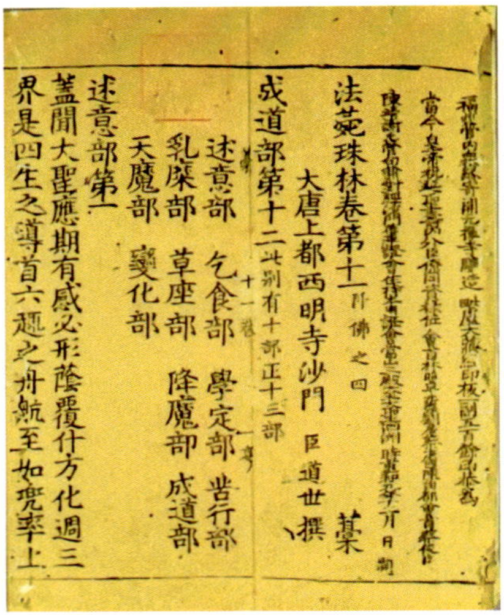
法菀珠林卷第十一
大唐上都西明寺沙門　臣道世撰
成道部第十二　此別有十部正十三部
述意部　乞食部　學定部　苦行部
乳糜部　草座部　降魔部　成道部
天魔部　變化部
述意部第一
蓋聞大聖應期有感必形蔭覆什方化遍三
界是四生之導首六趣之舟航至如兜率上

⦿ *Vairocana Buddhist Canon* of Kaiyuan Temple in Fuzhou, sample page (2), collected by Waseda University, Japan

⦿ Archives and Mausolea Department, Japan

2.3 The Cheng-Zhu School Spreads to the Korean Peninsula and Japan

In the Southern Song Dynasty, Zhu Xi took Fujian as his hometown of study. On top of ancient Chinese ideological and cultural achievements since Confucius, he digested and absorbed the essence of Fujian's local culture and formulated the Neo-Confucian worldview, also known as the Fujian School. During the Song, Yuan, Ming, and Qing Dynasties, his Neo-Confucianism was not only the prevailing consciousness and the major academic tradition of Chinese society, but also was introduced to the Korean Peninsula and the Japanese archipelago by scholars and officials at home and abroad, where it earned the admiration and respect of the ruling class.

As early as the Spring and Autumn period, Confucianism spread to the Korean Peninsula, where it was absorbed and respected by the rulers and intellectuals. The Cheng-zhu school was first introduced into the Korean Peninsula in 1288 by Ankyo of Goryeo.

⊙ The portrait of An Hyang

It was believed that Ankyo worshiped Zhu Xi tremendously, hanging the portrait of Zhu Xi on the wall of his house while using the character "Hui" in Zhu Xi's self-titled "Hui'an" as his title. To revitalize Confucianism in Goryeo, he proposed that officials above the sixth rank should donate half a kilo of silver currency and those below the seventh rank donate cloth to the Talent Program as a scholarship to encourage students to study and publicize the Cheng-zhu school. Meanwhile, he also sent a scholar Kim Wending to Yuan China to "draw the portraits of the sages and the seventy-two apprentices, and ask for sacrificial utensils, musical instruments, the Six Classics, and the history of the apprentices." All the efforts paved the way for the rapid development of Confucianism on the Korean Peninsula and the cultivation of a group of famous Confucian philosophers, such as Yi Hwang.

In the middle of the 13th century, the Cheng-Zhu school was brought to Japan by Zen monks and was widely spread. In the Tokugawa Shogunate period (1603–1867), it became the most authoritative value in Japanese society and politics.

⦿ The cover of Outline and Explanations of *The Works of Zhu Xi* by Yi Hwang, sample page

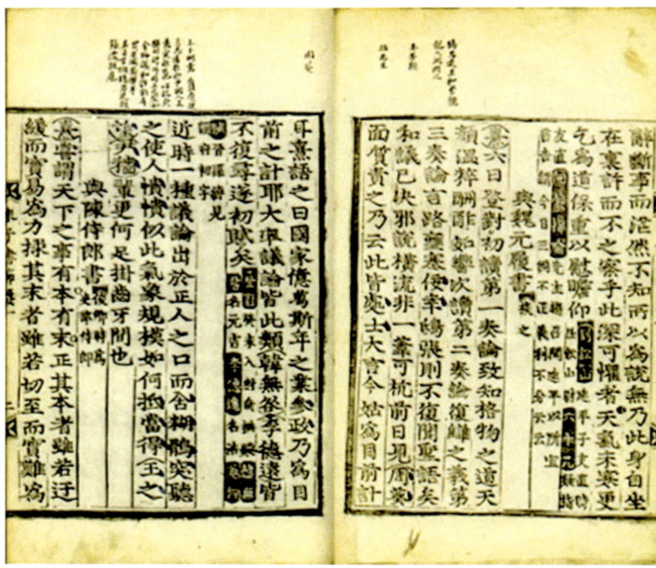

⦿ sample page of Outline and Explanations of *The Works of Zhu Xi*

The Cheng-Zhu school welcomed the heyday in the Ming and Qing Dynasties, during which there were Chinese constantly sailing to Japan. Especially, in the late Ming Dynasty and early Qing Dynasty, scholars were discontent with the reign of the Qing Dynasty and exiled themselves to Japan. In the process of exporting Chinese culture, the Cheng-Zhu school generated the most influence in Japanese ideological circles. One typical example was Zhu Shunshui's ambition to revive the Ming Dynasty, which inspired the idea of loyalty to the throne of Mito Domain and Kaga Domain. Eventually, it gave rise to the formation of Mito School.

⦿ The portrait of Zhu Shunshui

⦿ The memorial to the place where Zhu Shunshui died, located in the University of Tokyo, Japan

⦿ The portrait of Tokugawa Mitsukuni, collected by the History Gallery of Ibaraki Prefecture, Japan

2.4 Poetry of Mazu on the Korean Peninsula

The ancient countries on the Korean Peninsula kept close contact with China. During the reign of one emperor of the Ming Dynasty, there were 1,252 envoys from Goryeo, an average of 138 envoys to China on a yearly basis. Back then, the envoys of Goryeo had to travel by sea to China and back to their homeland. The journey used to involve a stay in the Mazu temples in Miaodao Archipelago and the Sancha River, where the monsoon would pass by. In awe of the goddess of peace on the sea from Fujian, they composed a great many poems glorifying Mazu.

Jeong Mong-ju (1337–1392) was sent on a diplomatic mission to China four times. He wrote a collection of poems called the *Poeun Collection*, the first volume of which contains the poem *Miaodao Archipelago*, which expresses his respect to Mazu and his hope for receiving her blessings.

⦿ Portrait of Jeong Mong-ju

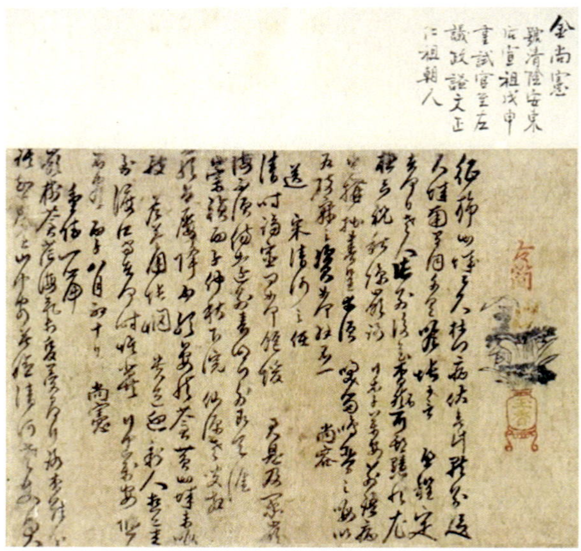

⦿ Calligraphy works by Kim Sang-heon

⊙ The Mazu Temple in the Miaodao Archipelago

Gwon Geun (1352–1409) was sent to China in 1389. On the fourth day of the ninth month of the Chinese lunar calendar, he and his entourage made a visit to the Mazu Temple in the Miaodao Archipelago to pay respect and pray for the wind. They wrote a poem *A Night in A Boat* to praise Mazu.

Yi Ch'ŏm (1345–1405) was twice sent to China. He wrote *Pray to Mazu, Cold Begone,* and *Waiting for the Wind on Miaodao Archipelago* to sing the praise of Mazu.

Wu Tianpo (1592–1634) was sent to China in July of 1624 and returned to Goryeo the next year. He was waiting for the wind to blow the way home at Miaodao Archipelago. And he wrote: "There is a temple of Mazu. To cross the sea safely, pray to her." The verse that lit the incense at the praising worship of Mazu in his poem *Waiting for the wind on Miaodao Archipelago* is proof that Mazu was worshipped on the Goryeo envoy ships back then.

Kim Sang-heon (1570–1652), who was sent to China in 1626 as Korea's envoy to express their gratitude, composed several poems when he was waiting for the wind on Miaodao Archipelago. Among them, *Chanting Mazu* was dedicated to the goddess.

2.5 Mazu Worship Spread to Japan

The unpredictable sea climate and turbulent currents increased the frequency of the occurrence of ancient shipwrecks. In the face of natural disasters, the ancestors could only pray for the protection of the gods, which bred the belief in the Gods of the sea. Mazu is one of them. Today, there are Mazu believers all over the world. Despite their residence in different foreign countries, they maintain a fraction of their national identity and spiritual dependence through Mazu worship.

Mazu belief spread to Japan as the trade of Fujian merchants reached Nagasaki.

There are Mazu halls in Nankin-dera Temple, Shōshū-dera Temple, and Fuku Shōshū-dera Temple in Nagasaki to worship Mazu statues and their subsidiary gods from China.

⦿ The Mazu hall in the Fujian Guild, Nagasaki, Japan

⦿ The statue of Mazu in the Ming and Qing Dynasties

⦿ The inside of the Mazu hall in Fujian Guild, Nagasaki, Japan

⦿ A statue of Mazu

⦿ A statue of Mazu

⦿ Clairvoyance

⦿ Front view

⦿ Side view

⦿ The statue of Mazu, Clairvoyance, and Clairaudience

⦿ Plaque

⦿ Chinese business people arriving at the port and heading towards the Mazu Temple in Tōjinyashiki (where Chinese resided) to place the Mazu statues

In addition, every Chinese merchant ship entering the Nagasaki port worshiped the Mother of Boats (a Bodhisattva Mazu on the ship), which would also be placed at the Mazu Hall of the Tang temples for temporary worship. A few months later, when the trade was finished, the statue would be taken out again before the merchant ships disembarked. The ceremony from taking the Mazu statue to the Tang Temples and inviting it back onboard is called *bosatsuage* in Japanese, which has been recorded in local literature as a unique custom of Nagasaki.

Annually, the grand lantern festival in Nagasaki prepares a contra dance performance of a ritual parade of Mazu. The grand performance recreates the scene of Chinese merchant ships berthing in Nagasaki during the Ming and Qing Dynasties and attracts countless visitors.

⦿ Mazu and imperial vehicle arrived at the main venue of Nagasaki Lantern Festival

⦿ One of the contra dances of Mazu at Nagasaki Latern Festival

⦿ Mazu statue presented by Meizhou Mazu temple to Nagasaki Lantern Festival

⦿ Dragon dance performance in front of Mazu Temple at Tōjinyashiki, collected by the Nagasaki Municipal Museum, Japan

⊙ The painting of performing in front of Mazu Temple in Tōjinyashiki, collected by the Nagasaki Municipal Museum, Japan

In addition to Nagasaki and Ryukyu, belief in Mazu is also found in some other places in Japan, such as Hirado, the Gōtō islands, Aomori, Chiba, Kanagawa, Osaka, and Hyogo in the pre-Edo period.

Belief in Mazu was localized when introduced to Japan. Mazu, integrated with the local Shinto tradition or worship of natural gods, gradually became the local aquatic guardian.

⦿ Mazu Statue in the Memorial Hall of Zheng Chenggong in Hirado, Japan (middle)

⦿ Mazu statue of the late Ming Dynasty preserved in Kyukawaguchi, Manosegawa, south Samatsu, Japan (middle)

⦿ Mazu statue in Tōjinmachi recorded in *Sho'nai Geographic Records*, Miyazaki Prefecture, Japan

⦿ Ototachibanahime Shrine in Mazu Mountain, Kitaibaraki-shi City, Ibaraki Prefecture, Japan

⊙ Tori

⊙ Eifukuji Temple in Tanoura, Kagoshima Prefecture, Japan, was a Mazu temple built by Chinese in the Edo period

2.6 Guan Yu in Japan

Holy Emperor Lord Guan is the title of Guangong Yu in Chinese folk religion. Since ancient times, there was the worship of Guan Yu wherever there were Chinese, from inland China to overseas. Guan Yu is the epitome of loyalty, faith and courage, trust, and the spirit of the business contract. Chinese business people widely embraced him as the God of Wealth. There are temples in Chinatowns in Nagasaki, Kobe, and Yokohama, that believe in Lord Guan.

⦿ The statue of Holy Emperor Lord Guan, collected by Shōfuku-ji Temple, Nagasaki, Japan

According to the Ming Dynasty work *Japan Atlas*, there are Lord Guan temples on the Gōtō Islands in the south of Kyushu, Japan. Evidently, as early as the 16th century, Fujian maritime merchants brought the belief in Lord Guan to the southwest of Kyushu when trading with Japan through the Gōtō Islands.

Subsequently, Chinese business people from Fujian, Guangdong, Jiangsu, and Zhejiang set up Lord Guan temples or statues in the three temples of the Tang Dynasty in Nagasaki, where worship ceremonies were held on a regular basis.

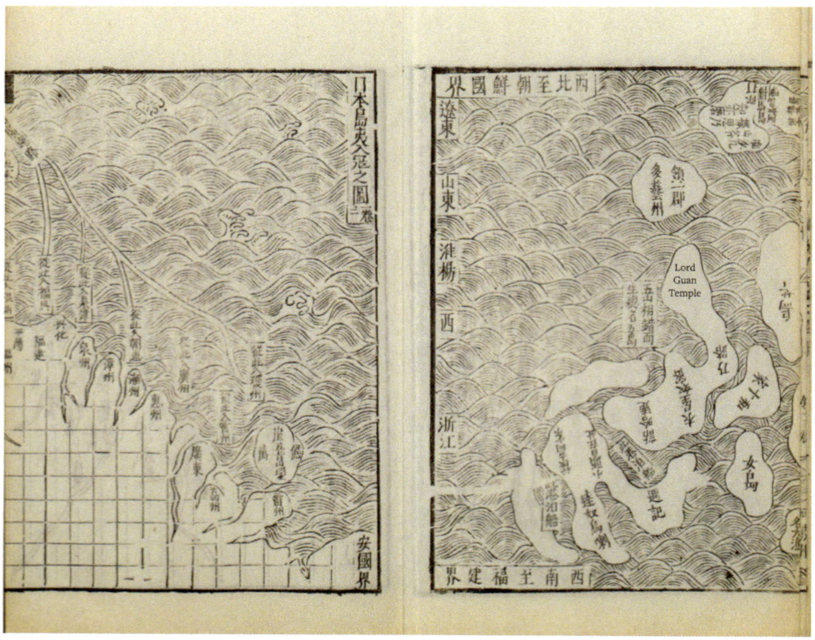

⦿ Lord Guan Temple on the the Gōtō Islands, Japan in the late Ming Dynasty recorded in *Japan Atlas*

⦿ Holy Emperor Lord Guan worshipped in the Dharma Chapel of Sōfuku-ji Temple in Japan

⦿ Lotus Hall of the old Fukusai-ji Temple in Nagasaki, Japan, where Holy Emperor Lord Guan was worshipped

At present, there are Lord Guan Temples in port cities such as Yokohama, Kobe, and Hakodate.

⊙ Exterior of the Lord Guan Temple in Yokohama, Japan around 1910

⊙ Today's Lord Guan Temple in Yokohama, Japan

⦿ Today's Lord Guan Temple in Kobe, Japan

⦿ The plaque that reads Tung Sin Tong Charitable Society in the Lord Guan Temple in Yokohama, Japan

⦿ The central hall of the Lord Guan Temple in the Chinese Guild in Hakodate, Japan

SUMMARY

Fujian's maritime merchants and monks, with no fear of difficulties and perils, crossed the ocean and created a sea route from Fujian to the countries in Northeast Asia with the help of ship-building techniques in the Fujian district. For thousands of years, trade has benefited the social economy of all countries along the sea route; and cultural exchanges have been rather fruitful and friendships have been bridged. Wherever we go today, in quiet Nagasaki or in bustling Pyongyang, in mysterious Kyoto or in thriving Seoul, footprints of the past are easily discovered. Buddhist temples, customs, social conduct, art, writings, and voices are all stamped with the mark of history between Fujian and the countries in Northeast Asia.

The history of maritime trade between Fujian and Northeast Asia is a significant part of the development of ancient China's Maritime Silk Road and an organic extension of an ancient Chinese foreign trade network. It is in these exchanges that Fujian and the people of all countries in Northeast Asia extended this maritime road today to the world.

REFERENCES

1. [Han] Ban Gu, *Book of the Later Han*, Zhonghua Book Company, 1965.
2. [Song] Zhao Rushi, *Yang Bowen's interpretation: Interpretation of A Description of Barbarian Nations, Records of Foreign People* (Zhu Fan ZHi), Zhonghua Book Company, 1996.
3. [Ming] Huang Zhongzhao, *General Records of Min*, Fujian People's Publishing House, 1989.
4. [Tang] Yao Silian, *Book of Liang*, Zhonghua Book Company, 1983.
5. [Chao] Jeong In-ji, *History of Goryeo*, Qilu Publishing House, 1996.
6. [Tang] Yijing, *Wang Bangwei's Annotation, Annotation of the Biography of the Eminent Monk Seeking Dharma in the Western Regions of the Tang Dynasty*, Zhonghua Book Company, 1988.
7. [Japan] Omino Mifune and annotated by Wang Xiangrong, *Legend of Jianzhen's Eastern Expedition*, Zhonghua Book Company, 1979.
8. [Japan] Kimiya Thai-yan, Anthony Woo, translation, *Japan-China Cultural Exchange History*, Commercial Press, 1980.
9. [Japan] Sato Nagato checked and annotated, *Biographies of Five Monks Tang Dynasty*, Takashi College, Japan, 2015.
10. [Japan] Hanawa Hokiichi, *Great Collection of Old Documents*, Japan Economic Journal, 1911.
11. [Japan] Fujiwara no Sanesuke, *Shōyūki, The 10th Century*, collected by the compilation of historical materials of University of Tokyo.
12. [Japan] Saeki Ariyoshi, *Six National Histories*, Asahi News Agency, 1940.
13. [Song] Xu Jing, *Xuanhe Envoy to Goryeo*, Commercial Press, 1937.
14. [Ming] He Qiaoyuan, *Book of Min*, Fujian People's Publishing House, 1994.

15. [Ming] Huang Huai and Yang Shiqi, *Memorials to Famous Ministers of Past Dynasties*, Taiwan Student Book Company, 1985.
16. [Song] Zhao Yanwei, *Yun Lu Man Chao*, Zhonghua Book Company, 1996.
17. [Yuan] Tuotuo et al. *History of the Song Dynasty*, Zhonghua Book Company, 1985.
18. [Japan] Ishizaki Yūshi, the drawings volume of the *Tulan of the Tang Dynasty*, Nagasaki Literature Society, 2001.
19. [Japan] Ōba Osamu, *Illutration Collection of Nagasaki Tang Museum*, Institute of East West studies, Kansai University, Japan, 2003.
20. *Compilation of Mazu Documents and Historical Materials*, edited by Chinese Mazu Cultural Exchange Association, etc. China Achives Press, 2007.
21. Wu Han, *Historical Materials of China in the Records of the Lee Dynasty in Korea*, Zhonghua Book Company, 1980.
22. Hong Huawen, editor in chief, *Complete Anthology of Yan Xing Lu (Volume I)*, Guangxi Normal University Press, 2010.
23. [Ming] *Records of Quanzhou in Wanli Years*, printed in 1869.
24. [Ming] Zheng Ruozeng et al. *Chou Hai Tu Bian*, printed in 1562, the 41st year of Jiajing in the Ming Dynasty.
25. [Ming] Zheng Shungong, *A Look at Japan*, published in 1939.
26. [Ming] Yao Shilin, *Jian Zhi Bian*, Taiwan Commercial Press, 1982.
27. [Ming] Mao Yuanyi, *Wu Bei Zhi, Qing Daoguang Movable Type Edition.*
28. [Japan] Nishikawa Joken, *Supplement of Kai Tsūshōkō*, collected by the Library of the Congress of Japan, 1695.
29. *Fujian Society and the Rural Economy in the Ming and Qing Dynasties*, edited by Fu Yiling and Yang Guozhen, Xiamen University Press, 1987.
30. Tang Wenji, editor in chief, *Fujian Ancient Economic History*, Fujian Education Press, 1994.
31. Liao Dake, *History of Fujian's Overseas Exchanges*, Fujian People's Publishing House, 2002.
32. *General History of Fujian*, edited by Xu Xiaowang, Fujian People's Publishing House, 2006.

About the Chief Editor

Mr. Xie Bizhen, Professor and Doctoral Supervisor of Fujian Normal University, Director of the Fujian-Taiwan Regional Research Center of Fujian Normal University, a key research base of humanities and social sciences of the Ministry of Education. His main research focuses on Chinese overseas transportation and trade history, the history of Sino-Japanese relations, and the local history of Fujian.

About the Authors

Mr. Xu Bin, Master of Economics from the National University of Ryukyu, Japan, Doctor of History from Fujian Normal University, associate researcher at the Fujian-Taiwan Regional Research Center of Fujian Normal University, a key research base of humanities and social sciences of the Ministry of Education, and master's supervisor. His research focuses on historical Sino-Ryuku relations and regional culture of Fujian and Taiwan. He has published numerous papers in *Research on the War of Resistance Against Japan, Fujian Forum, Journal of the Pacific, Journal of Fujian Normal University*, and *Research on the History of Maritime Transportation.*

Mrs. Zhang Jinhong, Doctor of History, lecturer at the School of Social History of Fujian Normal University. Her main research is on the history of Sino-foreign relations and the history of Christianity. She has published multiple papers in *Fujian Forum, Research on the History of Maritime Transportation, and Fujian Literature and History.*